New Regional Initiatives in China's Foreign Policy

Matteo Dian · Silvia Menegazzi

New Regional Initiatives in China's Foreign Policy

The Incoming Pluralism of Global Governance

palgrave
macmillan

Matteo Dian
Department of Political and Social Sciences
University of Bologna
Bologna, Italy

Silvia Menegazzi
Department of Political Science
LUISS Guido Carli University
Rome, Italy

ISBN 978-3-030-09249-8 ISBN 978-3-319-75505-2 (eBook)
https://doi.org/10.1007/978-3-319-75505-2

Printed on acid-free paper

This Palgrave Macmillan imprint is published by the registered company Springer International Publishing AG part of Springer Nature
The registered company address is: Gewerbestrasse 11, 6330 Cham, Switzerland

Acknowledgements

Many people offered advices and encouragement for this research project. First of all, we would like to thank the Finnish Institute of International Affairs that allowed us to present a first draft of this project in October 2015, and in particular Elina Sinkonnen for inviting us at the China Research Days workshop. In February 2016 we presented a second draft, related to the chapters on the theoretical framework and the AIIB at the China Centre, Oxford University. We are particularly in debt to Rosemary Foot for helping us to organize and hosting the seminar and offering important suggestions on the research.

Furthermore, we wish to thank Shaun Breslin, for offering relevant comments in the early stage of this research and Mark Beeson and Mario Telò, whose comments at the ISA 2016 convention in Hong Kong were particularly useful to structure our chapter in the manuscript on the Regional Comprehensive Economic Partnership.

Matteo Dian gratefully acknowledges Korea Foundation for the funding provided under the Next Generation Policy Experts programme.

Contents

1 **China in Regional and Global Governance and "Order Transition" in Asia** 1
Order Transitions and Primary Institutions. A Theoretical Framework 1
Regional Orders and Primary Institutions 4
Types of International Order 5
Regional Orders and the Global Order 7
Great Power Management 10
Geography and Spatial Definition of the Region 13
Sovereignty 15
State Capitalism, Contesting the Market as a Primary Institution 17
Bibliography 21

2 **The Origin of China's Ideational Narratives** 25
Introduction 25
Post-colonial Nationalism and Neo-Confucianism 28
A Dream for China 33
A New Type of International Relations 35
A New Model of Global Governance 39
Conclusion 41
Bibliography 43

3 **The Asian Infrastructure Investment Bank** 47
Introduction 47
AIIB: The Regional Order and Global Governance 50
The Chinese Narrative: AIIB as a New Type of International Financial Institution 53
AIIB: Structures and Operating Rules 55
Projects 58
AIIB Amid (Chinese) Sovereignty and State Capitalism 61
Conclusion 63
Bibliography 64

4 **Belt and Road, State Capitalism and China's Economic Interests** 67
The Chinese Narrative and the BRI 67
Belt and Road, State Capitalism and China's Economic Interests 70
Belt and Road, Geopolitics and the Regional Order 79
A Few Bumps Ahead for the Belt and Road 81
Conclusion 86
Bibliography 90

5 **The Regional Comprehensive Economic Partnership (RCEP)** 95
The Origin and the Changing Purpose of the RCEP 95
Economic Integration and the Chinese Narrative 98
The Content of the Regional Comprehensive Economic Partnership (RCEP) 101
SOEs, Market and State Capitalism 108
Conclusion 111
Bibliography 113

6 **Conclusion** 119
Bibliography 131

Index 133

CHAPTER 1

China in Regional and Global Governance and "Order Transition" in Asia

Abstract This chapter will propose a theoretical framework aimed at analysing the evolving role of the People's Republic of China in the processes of regionalization in Asia drawn from the English School approach to international relations. The rise of a new power in a region entails a process of contestation, adaptation and renegotiation of the main primary institutions of an international (or regional) order. In this case this chapter would consider several of the key primary institution that are subject to a process of renegotiation due to the rise of China in Asia: Great power management; Territoriality as a geographical or spatial definition of the region; Sovereignty; Market.

Keywords China · Regionalism · East Asia · English School
International order · Primary institutions

Order Transitions and Primary Institutions. A Theoretical Framework

China's recent regional initiatives represent a fundamental lens through which we can analyze and understand Beijing's rapidly evolving role in the regional and global order.

Thirty years ago, Deng Xiaoping theorized the need to avoid any leadership role in Asia, in order to concentrate on domestic reforms and modernization (Vogel 2011). Since the rise to power of Xi Jinping and

M. Dian and S. Menegazzi, *New Regional Initiatives in China's Foreign Policy*, https://doi.org/10.1007/978-3-319-75505-2_1

the Fifth Generation of Leaders, China has proposed a comprehensive blueprint aimed at transforming regional governance in Asia.[1] The objective of reforming and integrating the current regional and global economic order led to the promotion of the three most relevant initiatives of the Xi era: the Belt and Road initiative (BRI); the Asia Infrastructure and Investment Bank (AIIB) and the Regional Comprehensive Economic Partnership (RCEP). This plan has the potential to trigger a substantial evolution for the contemporary economic order, regionally and globally, and to redefine the Chinese role in Asia and beyond.

This book aims to analyse the origins, content and possible consequences of China's regional blueprint, and the three flagship initiatives associated with it. The book will employ a theoretical framework drawn from the English School or International Society approach to international relations, especially from recent theoretical developments that incorporate issues such as power shifts and order transitions, when considering the Asian context. This framework has several advantages. Firstly, it eschews the two main Manichaean narratives that have characterized mainstream International Relations (IR) theories relating to the rise of China: the realist narrative, which predicts a future of security competition between China and the other key Asian states, and the liberal integrationist narrative, which underlines the capacity of the global order to socialize and include a new great power through economic and social means.

Realists and power transition theorists have emphasized how Beijing's ascendency, as with the rise of other great powers in the past, is likely to generate instability and security competition, and even trigger a hegemonic war (Friedberg 1993; Mearsheimer 2010). Structural realists tend to consider contemporary China as a potential hegemon for East Asia. As a result, according to these interpretations, a rising China will, whether or not it means to do so, destabilize the present regional order, create instability, and threaten its neighbours (Kirshner 2010). From this perspective, China and the United States (US), are likely to fall into the Thucydides' trap (Allison 2017): as the Ancient Greek historian stated about the conflict between Athens and Sparta, it was "the rise of Athens and the fear that this inspired in Sparta that made war inevitable"

[1] Xi Jinping and Li Keqiang are considered to be part of the Fifth Generation of Leaders in the Peoples' Republic. The first generation was identified with Mao Zedong, the second with Deng Xiaoping, the third with Jiang Zemin, and the fourth with Hu Jintao.

(Gilpin 1984, p. 289). Similarly, Beijing's ascent would create a competition for security and primacy between Beijing, as a new rising power, and the US.

Analyses inspired by constructivist and liberal theories have generally provided less pessimistic predictions. They have indicated how several factors, from economic interdependence to institutionalization of the contemporary order, are likely to prevent a hegemonic conflict. Liberal theorists, such as John Ikenberry, have highlighted how China has been growing within the system, and has realized that it is much easier to join the current liberal international order rather than trying to subvert it (Ikenberry 2008). Other liberal analyses have illustrated how the important level of economic, commercial and financial integration have prevented the US and China from engaging in a great power competition. Others have located the possibility of a peaceful rise to the broader framework of a capitalist peace (Weede 2010).

Constructivist analyses have underlined how Beijing has been socialized by its participation in the vast array of international institutions and regimes that underpin the current order (Johnston 2008). Other analyses, inspired both by the constructivist and the liberal perspective, have argued that the Chinese rise represents a factor of stability and peace for the region. David Kang highlighted how the Beijing ascendency was above all a return to normality for the region (Kang 2008). Other Asian states, according to Kang, are likely to consider it both as an opportunity for trade and economic development and a return to a natural situation, after a long interlude, which began with the demise of the empire and culminated in the prolonged period of self-isolation following the Maoist revolution (Kang 2010).

The English School of International Relations has provided several interesting theoretical insights on the rise of China that overcome the Manichaean contraposition between the realist and liberal perspectives. The English School considers the rise of a new great power, such as China, as the origin of both a power shift (namely, a redistribution of material capabilities) and a process of order transition—a process of renegotiation of the patterns of hierarchy in the regional order, and the normative content of the order itself. The rise of a new power in a region entails a process of contestation, adaptation and renegotiation of the normative roots of an international (or regional) society (Goh 2013; Buzan and Zhang 2014a).

In contrast with early constructivist accounts, China is not simply the subject of a process of socialization through which it absorbs rules and norms of the international order. It can also promote its own norms and its own ideas concerning key institutions of the international society. This dialectic between assimilation and contestation represents a fundamental theoretical and analytical insight, since it helps to avoid an over-simplistic and dichotomist choice between postulating the logical necessity of the Thucydides trap and theorizing a unidirectional and unproblematic process of socialization and homogenization (Zhang 2011; Buzan 2010). This approach, focusing on the dynamic between socialization, contestation and resistance, is capable of describing and theorizing a fundamental effect of the Chinese ascendency and of the contemporary order transition: the process of influence and socialization has been mutual. China has been socialized according to the norms and institutions of the Western-led international order. However, China is demonstrating itself as increasingly capable of shaping the normative and institutional foundations of the order, regionally and globally.

Regional Orders and Primary Institutions

The crucial and perhaps most distinctive concept of the English School approach is that of primary institutions. In our analysis, primary institutions are central to an understanding how and to what extent China's regional initiatives are leading to a process of renegotiation of the current regional order in Asia.

The English School literature has indicated several key features of primary institutions. As stated by Hedley Bull, in his classic account: "By an institution we do not necessarily imply an organisation or administrative machinery, but rather a set of habits and practices shaped towards the realisation of common goals." (Bull 1977, p. 74). Barry Buzan later specified the concept further, defining the fundamental properties of primary institutions as "durable and recognised patterns of shared practices rooted in values held commonly by the members of interstate societies, and embodying a mix of norms, rules and principles" (Buzan 2004, p. 181). Importantly, these norms, rules and practices should be shared and considered as legitimate by members of the international society. Primary institutions constitute the fundamental normative pillar of an international order. As a result, they represent a crucial constraint to asymmetry of economic, political and military power.

Primary institutions, moreover, “play a constitutive role in relation to both the pieces/players and the rules of the game” (ibid.). They are durable but not permanent. They rise, they evolve, and they can decline. While primary institutions such as dynasticism and colonialism disappeared during the last century, norms, values and practices related to equality of people, such as self-determination and human rights, have risen and evolved, determining a fundamental change in contemporary international politics.

The original list of primary institutions proposed by Hedley Bull included diplomacy, war, balance of power, great power management, and international law. Contemporary literature broadly agrees to consider as fundamental primary institutions sovereignty, territoriality, diplomacy, great power management, equality of people, market, nationalism, and environmental stewardship.

Types of International Order

The English School literature generally identifies two ideal types of international order: pluralist and solidarist (Buzan 2014). Pluralist orders are defined by the prevalence of the role and the rights of states. Moreover, they are characterized by a normative orientation that gives priority to the necessity of order over the research of justice. An ideal-typical pluralist order is rooted in the respect of sovereignty and non-interference; it assigns a prominent role to great powers as keepers of the international stability; international law primarily delimits the interactions between states. The ideal type of pluralist order is very close to a Westphalian international system, in which states are sovereign in their own territory, and do not seek to interference in the domestic politics of other states.

As suggested by Hurrell, in a pluralist order, while states recognize the presence of common as well as diverging interests, they realize that cooperation is hard to achieve. Therefore, cooperation is limited to the management of problems that endanger their coexistence, such as nuclear proliferation, and conflict limitation (Hurrell 2007). Finally, and importantly for our analysis, a pluralist order is, by definition, open to ideological differences, especially as every state has the right to self-determination.

By contrast, solidarist orders are defined by the priority assigned to the protection of the rights of individuals and the promotion of justice, beyond the limits of the sovereignty of a state and non-interference in the affairs of other states. Moreover, solidarist orders are defined by "high, or wide, degree of shared norms, rules and institutions among states" (Buzan 2004, p. 49). In a solidarist order, the international community, states and especially great powers, have a duty to advance and protect the rights of individuals beyond the limits of a state's sovereignty (Linklater 1998). In a solidarist order, human rights and individual integrity should also be upheld through the practice of humanitarian interventions, and the application of the doctrine of Responsibility to Protect (R2P). International law and global governance should transcend the limits of state's sovereignty. Multilateralism is considered a more legitimate and viable instrument for international policymaking than bilateralism. International institutions have the right and the duty to intervene, directly regulating issues related to the economic, social and political sphere.

Even if the English School literature does not generally emphasize this issue, here it is important to include free trade and the globalization of capitalism among the crucial elements of a contemporary solidarist order. In an ideal-typical free market, individuals, as with economic agents, are free to produce, trade, invest and purchase despite and beyond national boundaries. As a consequence, international law and global governance should protect their rights to do so globally, limiting obstacles put in place by states to hinder free economic activities, or to make production, trade or finance an instrument functional to the national interest.

This distinction between the solidarist and the pluralist ideal type is crucial for analyzing the role of China in the contemporary regional and global order, as well for understanding the normative orientation that has been influencing China's regional initiatives. As this book will argue, Beijing's attempts to contest and reshape the international order can often be understood as an effort to resist the development of solidarist elements in the contemporary international order, while reaffirming the pluralist and "Westphalian" elements.

The book will explore how China's identity and foreign policy practices have been, and remain, intertwined with a substantially pluralist vision of international politics and a resistance to the majority of the attempts of solidarist elements being injected into the international order. In Chapter 2, we will describe the origins of the main ideas that have underpinned China's recent regional initiatives. Concepts such as the new type of great power relations, win-win relations, and, to a certain extent, the "Chinese Dream", are strongly associated with a pluralist, if not a Westphalian, orientation.

Regional Orders and the Global Order

Another relevant theoretical issue for our analysis is the relationship between regions, regional orders and global order (Stivachtis 2015). From an English School perspective, regions cannot be considered "natural", or a by-product of geographical proximity. Regional orders entail different elements: some level of regionalization, defined by the existence of a degree of societal integration and networks of economic, political and societal exchanges; the presence of interstate political cooperation that generally corresponds with the existence of international or sovranational institutions; finally, a degree of regional identity or regional awareness. In other terms, regions are socially and politically constructed by agents, who act to construct a sense of belonging or identification.

The first generation of English School scholarship explained the historical existence of the regional orders and regions by the fact that the expansion of European and Western international society was uneven. As a result, different regions absorbed, via socialization or imposition, the fundamental primary institutions of the international society at different times and in different degrees. These accounts underline how decolonization represented the ultimate manifestation of the expansion of the European international society (Bull and Watson 1984; Watson 1992).

More recent accounts have criticized the Eurocentric bias of these earlier ones, highlighting the role of non-Western agents in absorbing, promoting, localizing or resisting key primary institutions that originated in the West (Hobson 2012). The theoretical point made by this second wave of scholarship is crucial for our analysis. The "expansion perspective" considers the return of China to international society after 1978 as a one-sided and uneven process of socialization to the normative core of the Western-led global international order. However, our analysis will underline how China has not only grown capable of resisting undesired evolutions pointing towards a solidarist order, but has also been developing the capacity to promote its own vision of the regional order, rooted in its own principles and its own narrative.

The relationship between the global order and its normative foundations and the regional order and local primary institutions is central to our analysis. From an English School perspective, the relationship between regions and the global international society revolves around four main elements: (1) regions are containers for normative diversity and difference; (2) regions are poles built around power asymmetries;

(3) regions entail levels in a system of multilevel global governance; and (4) regions are harbingers of change in the character of international society (Hurrell 2007, p. 239).

The first point touches upon the fundamental role of primary institutions. As Buzan and Zhang have stated, the key to identifying the existence of a regional order is in identifying the level of differentiation from the global order and its Western normative core, the degree of differentiation from the neighbouring regional order, and its placement on the pluralist–solidarist spectrum (Buzan and Zhang 2014b).

Consequently, regional orders can manifest primary institutions that are not present at global level, they can lack primary institutions present at global level, or they can interpret them differently, displaying significantly different practices associated with them. This differentiation, which generally manifests itself through processes of resistance and contestation, is probably the most common, as well as the most relevant (Costa-Buranelli 2015).

The European Union (EU) is an example of differentiation in a solidarist sense. It has promoted an attempt to overcome the fundamental pluralist and Westphalian elements of international society, through the abolition of internal borders, the development of a multi-layered citizenship (national and European), and transcendence of national sovereignty and non-interference (Stivachtis and Webber 2015). Conversely, the East Asian regional order has moved in the opposite direction, with China as well as the Association of Southeast Asian Nations (ASEAN) members working towards the reinforcement of sovereignty and non-interference as a fundamental normative pillar for the region.

The existence of a regional order involved the translation of a hierarchy of power into a working local order. This in turn necessitates two elements: the translation of asymmetric power into legitimate authority, and the achievement of solution to common problems both in the realm of security and economic cooperation. Finally, a regional order tends to generate a regional level of governance and regional institutions. These institutions can be inspired by what Acharya has defined as local normative prior, namely reflecting local norms and values, or reflecting a negotiated compromise between local and global norms (Acharya 2011). For instance, cooperation within ASEAN tends to reflect the respect of sovereignty generally associated with an "Asian" and post-colonial collective prior. However, economic cooperation in the realm of ASEAN+3 could be considered as a compromise between global and local norms in terms of monetary and financial regulations.

Finally, the evolution of a regional order is a harbinger for change in the global order. A process of contestation and evolution at the regional level can determine a movement towards more solidarism or more pluralism, and can make the global order more homogenous or more heterogeneous in terms of values, norms and practices. In this sense, China's effort to promote a regional order based on its own leadership and Chinese values represents a fundamental evolution for the international order in the direction of pluralism and heterogeneity.

For a number of reasons, these concepts are crucial for our analysis of China's recent regional initiatives for. Firstly, this book will explore how China's regional blueprint is a fundamental element of an order transition, namely the attempt to build a regional order that, if not isolated from the global order, is increasingly underpinned by China's centrality as well as its interests and values. China is, in fact, the most outspoken supporter of the idea of normative difference, and has championed the idea of a global order in which different powers and different regions can find their own recipe for modernity and development. In doing so, China represents a crucial counterweight to the attempts promoted by the US, but more generally in the West, to push the global order in a clearly solidarist direction.

The English School literature has often underlined this trend in the dimension of security, with the rise of the doctrine of humanitarian intervention and ultimately R2P. It is important to highlight that this trend is also relevant in the economic realm. Western capitalist globalization is comparable to a solidarist trend, since it put individuals and firms at the heart of the system, recognizing their rights beyond the boundaries of state powers and borders. In this sense, the rise of China, and the Chinese attempt to reform the regional order represents a crucial form of resistance to these developments and a clear re-affirmation of the right of the state to use the economy to pursue political goals.

This theoretical background provides us with a particular lens through which to analyse China's role in the region, as well as its attempt to promote its values and interests regionally and globally. In order to understand the origin, scope and consequences of regional initiatives such as AIIB, BRI and RCEP, we should understand how they are related to the process of order transition. Therefore, it is important to understand the extent to which they aim to contribute to the process of differentiation between the regional and global order, reinforcing China's role as regional leader.

In order to analyse this process, we will look mainly at four primary institutions: great power management; territoriality, as spatial definition of the boundaries of the region; sovereignty; and market. Here, we assume that the regionalist project started under Xi Jinping involves an attempt to contest, at least to some degree, each of them. In the following section, we will introduce the main features of these primary institutions and explain why we consider them to be at the centre of China's attempt to promote its own vision of the regional order.

Great Power Management

The concept of great power management is related to a key insight of the English School: the idea that political order is not simply a by-product of distribution of power, but requires a process of social recognition. The status of great power involves several rights and responsibilities. According to Bull's original definition, "Great powers contribute to international order by maintaining local systems of hegemony within which order is imposed from above, and by collaborating to manage the global balance of power and, from time to time, to impose their joint will on others." (Bull 1977, p. 196).

As Loke has pointed out, great power management is dual in nature. It is defined by a horizontal dimension, constituted by the necessity to limit conflict between the great powers themselves, and a vertical dimension embodied by the orchestration of international affairs between the great powers as an elite directorate and the rest of international society (Loke 2016). The expectations about what a great power should do to see its status recognized vary according to the type of order in which it operates. In an ideal-typical pluralist order, expectations would be limited to the prevention of conflict. In a solidarist order, the duties of great powers would extend to the protection of human rights, the promotion of global governance, and of international trade.

Ultimately, the recognition of the status of great power is incidental and it is not related to superior capabilities alone. It is also related to the capacity to translate asymmetry of power in legitimacy. This, in turn, depends on several elements, such as the capacity to provide public goods, include other states in the management of the order, and provide solutions to problems of cooperation and coordination in key sectors such as security and economic governance (Goh 2014).

Great power management is based on a social process and a process of self-identification. This means that (1) great powers should be recognised as such by other states and especially by other great powers; and (2) great powers should recognize their own special status. Consequently, it is important to think about the possibility of a disconnection between self-perception and recognition. A state that considers itself as a great power, but lacks recognition by others, is likely to be perceived as a revisionist. In the case of a partial disconnection between self-perception and recognition, a state would be recognized as promoter of a process of contestation of certain elements of the international or regional order. This is probably the case with contemporary China, which accepts many elements of the current order, but aims to be recognized as a leader of the regional order in Asia.

Several scholars have underlined how, during the post-Cold War period, great power management as primary institutions was strongly underdeveloped, especially when compared to other regions. For instance, Yongjin Zhang described the "abject failure of indigenous powers, China and Japan, as either providers or managers of regional order in East Asia", noting that "two regional great powers have not even managed to develop a shared notion of coexistence or cooperation, not to speak of jointly providing leadership in defining and stabilizing regional order through cultivating shared norms and values" (Zhang 2015, p. 368). The fact that the Japan and China did not reach a compromise on fundamental issues, including the limitation of conflict, the recognition of each other's status, and the necessity to jointly work at the resolution of problems of coordination, led to several distinctive consequences. Firstly, an "upward" delegation of the function of great power management to the US; secondly, a "downward" delegation to ASEAN, as a promoter of local regional initiatives; and finally, a process of "institutional racing" between China and Japan.

For several reasons, the concept of great power management is central to our analysis. Here, it is necessary to return to the notion of great power management as a product of a process of self-identification and a process of mutual social recognition. Mutual social recognition between great powers in East Asia is likely to remain relatively underdeveloped in the foreseeable future. Mutual social denial between China and Japan has both favoured the maintenance of a crucial role for the US and generated an oversupply of regional (secondary) institutions. These trends are not likely to disappear overnight. However, it is important to recognize that the comprehensive blueprint for the regional order proposed by the current Chinese leadership represents a relevant attempt to promote a new version of great power management for East Asia and Asia more broadly. China has increasingly identified itself and promoted itself as the leader and the "order maker" of the region. This has generated a process of contestation regarding roles, expectations and perceptions of appropriate behaviour.

The Chinese blueprint for the region is defined both by ideas on the horizontal and the vertical dimensions of great power management. The first includes concepts such as new types of great power relations and, implicitly foresees a progressive reduction of the US presence in the region. The second designs an entirely new relationship between China and the other Asian countries. As we will describe in detail in the following chapters, Beijing has been promoting a vision of the regional order based both on respect for political, cultural and economic differences, and a renewed role of leadership for China itself.

The Chinese proposals are particularly focused on economic cooperation and development, while the security dimension remains relatively secondary.[2] This is a result of the recognition of the current security dynamics in the region, characterized by an intense security competition especially between Beijing and the US and its allies, particularly Japan and the Philippines.

Finally, great power management remains a relatively underdeveloped institution in East Asia. The rise of China, and more specifically the regionalist blueprint promoted by the current leadership, signals the intention to further contest the main tenets of the post-Cold War regional order. More specifically, Beijing has been promoting a model of regional order in which the American capacity to shape rules and norms has declined and China has assumed the role of order maker. Here, we don't assume that China's proposal will necessarily be successful and will fail to meet resistance. Key states such as Japan and South Korea, even if with some differences, are clearly in favour of an enduring role of the US. Vietnam is also likely to resist any development favouring a Chinese regional leadership. Nevertheless, the Chinese proposals have found a significant purchase in other parts of South East, South and Central Asia.

[2]The process of contestation promoted by China involves also the security dimension. The challenge to the maritime and territorial borders in the South and East China Sea can be interpreted also as an attempt to limit the US role in Asia.

Ultimately therefore, the Chinese regional blueprint should be considered as a sign of wider process of contestation regarding the fundamental rules and norms of the regional order. China has increasingly rejected the notion that great power management should be delegated upwards (to the US) and downwards to ASEAN. However, it has been advancing a model of order in which it occupies a leadership role, providing rules norms and principles for regional governance.

Geography and Spatial Definition of the Region

Territoriality and geography, defined as spatial definition of the political and social boundaries, represent another crucial dimension of our analysis. In the classic studies of the English School, the idea of territory as primary institutions refers primarily to the emergence of national borders as the main element of European international society. Here we don't refer to this notion of territoriality, but rather to the definition and the possible contestation of the social and political boundaries of a region.

As anticipated, our framework does not consider regions as "natural", namely simply defined by geography or political activities. Here, we build on the basic insight of critical geography, the assumption that "spatial scales can no longer be conceived as pre-given or natural areas of social interaction, but are increasingly viewed as historical products at once socially constructed and politically contested" (Brenner 1998, p. 466). Consequently, regions should be considered as constructed by politics and identity, with the possibility of transcending material borders and spatiality. As Söderbaum has stated, regions are "made, remade and unmade", in the process of global transformation and identity formation (Söderbaum 2014, p. 13).

Defining the degree of distinctiveness of a region in normative terms, as well as the geographical boundaries of this distinctiveness, is a crucial exercise in political power. In other words, the capacity to imagine a region, to define its boundaries and to shape its normative content, represent a fundamental exercise in hegemonic power in a Gramscian sense. The idea of social construction of space through practices, norms and identities entails the theoretical possibility of both exclusive and open regions. An exclusive region would be centred on the leadership of a leading state (or more than one), characterized by norms and values originating within the region, and relatively isolated from external influences. The Sino-centric system that characterized East Asia before Western colonialism can be considered as an example of exclusive regional order (Fairbank 1942; Zhang and Buzan 2012). Since the beginning of the Age of Discovery to the Opium Wars, the East Asian order survived as a distinctive regional order, in a period in which the European international society was expanding globally (Zhang 2014; Suzuki 2014). Before the decline and eventual collapse of the Qing Empire, the East Asian order was based on Chinese leadership and on a set of distinct and "local" primary institutions, such as the practice of tribute and a formal hierarchy among states. In contrast, post-Cold War East Asia can be considered as an open region, in which regional primary institutions are a product of a political bargaining between an external great power, the US, that exercises also a role of global leader, and local powers such as China, Japan and, to a lesser extent, ASEAN powers.

For two essential reasons, the process of redefining the geographical boundaries of the region is a crucial dimension of the order transition generated by the rise of China. Firstly, the role that Beijing designed for itself in the regional order fundamentally evolved from the late 1970s, going from complete alienation in the aftermath of the Maoist era, to an attempt to promote a Chinese leadership under Xi. During the Deng era, and during the first phase of Jiang Zemin's leadership, the Chinese leadership preferred to minimize any participation in regional governance, considering it a potential political constraint, or even a threat to Chinese sovereignty and self-determination. Only after the 1997–1998 crisis did the Chinese leadership start to consider the edification of forms of regional governance to build a limit to the power and influence of the US. In the period between the Asian Financial Crisis and the late 2000s, China started to consider the promotion of a regional order, based on local rules and values, a fundamental interest. It is important to note, however, that at the time, in contrast with today, Beijing did not present itself as a necessary centre or leader of a wider Asian region. On the one hand, it tried to promote forms of "East Asian" cooperation based on the ASEAN+3 framework. On the other hand, these forms of cooperation were undermined by the deterioration of bilateral relations with Tokyo (Bowles 2002; Beeson 2006). Finally, under the leadership of Xi Jinping, the Chinese leadership has advanced a new blueprint for the regional order, which constitutes the object of this book, and will be explored in detail in the following chapters. What it is important to clarify here is that the blueprint for regional order advanced by the Xi and the Fifth Generation of Leadership constitutes the final point of a process of redefining the social and political boundaries of Asia as a region and a regional order, as well as a process of re-thinking the Chinese role in it. As Chapter 2 will highlight, this process has been rooted in distinctively Chinese concepts. Moreover, it has been based on a long and sophisticated intellectual elaboration that has mixed ideas related to post-colonial nationalism and neo-Confucianism.

This blueprint for regional order generated a "clash of meanings" with the ideas on the regional order proposed by other key actors, such as the US and Japan (Goh 2013). The US have tried to promote an open "Asia-Pacific" form of regional order, based on the maintenance of the American leadership both in the realm of security and in the economic sphere. The Pivot to Asia, promoted by the Obama administration, was an example of the attempt to establish a wide regional order, rooted in US led hub and spoke security alliances, and Trans-Pacific institutions such as the Trans-Pacific Partnership (TPP). However, China has gradually elaborated an East Asian or even "Asian" model of regional order, based on the exclusion of the US and the Chinese centrality in a wider continental region, embracing Central, South, South East and East Asia.

Ultimately, the redefinition of the geographical boundaries of the regional order, embodied by the attempt to promote a new model of exclusive order, based on the centrality of China in the wider Asian continent, represents a crucial dimension of the analysis of Beijing regional initiatives.

Sovereignty

Sovereignty is one of the central primary institutions in every analysis inspired by the societal approach to IR. In the classic rendition of the English School, the rise of sovereignty as a central feature of international politics is an essential element both of the evolution of the European international society, and its expansion into the extra-European space in the age of colonialism (Bull and Watson 1984). In this sense, sovereignty is conceived, in a Weberian sense, as a monopoly of legitimate force over a given territory, and as non-recognition of any superior political authority. The crucial corollary of modern sovereignty is therefore the principle of non-interference in the domestic politics of other states. The international society as a system of states is rooted in the acceptance of the sovereign equality and non-interference in domestic politics. This makes sovereignty the conceptual keystone of pluralist orders, since it defines the superiority of the rights of the state over those of the individual.

What is more important from our perspective is to clarify how and why the concept of sovereignty is crucial for Asia and, in particular, for China. In order to do so, it is important to highlight the critique of the "expansion" theory proposed by most recent scholarship on the role of sovereignty in the post-colonial world. Both constructivists and English School theorists have highlighted how post-colonial states have played an active role both in their struggle to become sovereign and in their re-elaboration of sovereignty as a political concept (Acharya 2011; Zhang 2015).

The concept of sovereignty, from this perspective, is not a norm that post-colonial states absorbed from the West. Rather, it is the core norm stemming from the colonial experience and the struggle for independence. Therefore, for post-colonial states, sovereignty is conceptualized primarily as independence from colonial domination, self-determination, racial equality and formal parity with other states. As highlighted by Acharya and Ba, this divisively shaped the way in which post-colonial states approached international cooperation and, more specifically, regionalism. While the European experience is defined by the idea of transcending sovereignty, post-colonial states sought forms of cooperation aimed to strengthen their sovereignty from external interference. For instance, the Treaty of Amity and Cooperation in South East Asia, signed in 1976, states that "Mutual respect for the independence, sovereignty, equality, territorial integrity and national identity of all nations" and that "The right of every State to lead its national existence free from external interference, subversion or coercion" (ASEAN 2016).

The idea of "sovereignty confirming" forms of cooperation had already emerged during the period leading to the Bandung Conference and decisively informed China's contribution to the Five Principles of Peaceful Co-existence. These principles, especially after the Maoist period, became core guiding principles for Beijing's foreign policy. They have been enshrined in the Constitution since 2004 and are included in virtually every bilateral treaty signed by China. As stated by Yongjin Zhang:

> China defends a pluralist international order that gives the state ontological priority. [...] This defence is informed, in important part, by China's

> own experience of nation-state building and its encounter with expanding European international society in the late nineteenth and early twentieth century. For China, the sovereign state and the associated principle of the inviolability of state sovereignty remain the best available instrument and hope for the protection of its national security against foreign invasion and external threat in the anarchical society of states. (Zhang 2016, p. 801)

This does not mean that China tries to practice and promote sovereignty in its pure, Westphalian and ideal-typical form. On the contrary, as underlined by Rosemary Foot, among others, China has become open to the human rights regime and has made some limited and tactical concessions to the doctrine of R2P (Foot 2011). These positions, however, do not alter the Chinese preference towards a pluralist order. China remains firmly in opposition to solidarist developments, both regionally and globally (Permanent Mission of the PRC to the UN 2009).[3]

Therefore, from the perspective of this research, it is crucial to understand how China-led regional initiatives can be used by Beijing to promote a regional order embedded in pluralist roots and how AIIB, BRI, and RCEP can be considered as "sovereignty confirming" forms of cooperation.

State Capitalism, Contesting the Market as a Primary Institution

The market is a crucial primary institution for the analysis of the evolving Chinese role in the region and globally. Here, it is important to underline three basic points. Firstly, we need to clarify why it is crucial to recognize the market as a primary institution. Secondly, it is essential to distinguish between the two fundamental ideal-types of market as a primary institution. In turn, these are associated with the two key models of order that characterize contemporary East Asia: the US-led Asia-Pacific model, which includes several solidarist features, and the Sino-centric model, closer to the pluralist ideal-type. Finally, it is relevant to recognize how and why China has been contesting the market as a primary institution, in particular, how China has promoted its own version of the market.

[3]The Chinese government stated in 2006 that R2P should not 'contravene the principle of state sovereignty and the principle of non-interference of internal affairs'.

The market qualifies as a primary institution, since it can be described as "a fundamental and durable practice, which is constitutive of actors and their patterns of legitimate activity in relation to each other" (Buzan 2004, p. 167). This definition touches upon a fundamental issue regarding this research, namely understanding which practices are considered as legitimate in the field of economic policies, and how they contribute to shape the behaviour of the actors. This is crucial for the analysis of China's regional initiative, since Beijing is advancing a rather unique model of economic development, centred on a peculiar relationship between political power and economic agents.

Aside from the recognition of the market as a primary institution, the English School has very rarely engaged systematically with the concept or more generally with the economic dimension of the international order (Buzan and Lawson 2015). However, the literature on the subject has produced two key insights. Firstly, the expansion of the international society has led Asian states to embrace "the market", and become part of the global capitalist economic system. This culminated in the Chinese economic reforms and the end of the Cold War. The second key point regards the different role of the state in the economy in Asian states, compared to Europe and the West. In this case, the export-oriented model of developmental state is generally presented as the key feature of the Asian type of market. Other analyses, following the insights of the literature on Varieties of Capitalism, have argued that most East and South East Asian states adopted the model of Coordinated Market Economy (Hall and Soskice 2001). These analyses highlight the role of Japan as a model for late developers, such as Taiwan, South Korea and South East Asian states, and ultimately for China.

The Varieties of Capitalism Approach captures several of the key differences between the various types of capitalism, stressing the relevance of different models of coordination. The Chinese model displays a number of features typical of a Coordinated Market Economy, such as the centrality of banks for credit provision, corporate governance oriented on long-term market shares, the priority given to exports over domestic consumption, and a high level of coordination between firms (Naughton and Tsai 2015).

However, here we argue that, at least for our analytical purposes, the different types of coordination do not explain the entire peculiarity of the Chinese ideas of market, nor do they define the distinctiveness of the "clash of meanings" between liberal market capitalism and Chinese

State Capitalism. The crucial difference can be defined in relation of the two main ideal-types of international order. Free market capitalism in its advanced form should be considered as a solidarist element of the order. Here, by solidarist, we don't mean that the expansion of free markets necessarily promotes human justice and morality. Here, solidarist means that the expansion of free markets necessarily generates an erosion of the centrality of the state as a basic pillar of the international order *vis-à-vis* the rights of individuals and firms.

Globalization of market forces reduces the capacity of sovereign states to impose their will over markets, to regulate fluxes of capitals, or even to have autonomous fiscal, monetary, industrial and commercial policies. Even more crucially, embracing free market capitalism reduces the capacity to use economic policies as an instrument to promote national interests. As a result, advanced forms of governance inspired a liberal market model aim to protect the economic rights of individuals and to curb the capacity of states to control economic dynamics. The proliferation of "behind the borders" issues, and the vast array of rules aimed overcome non-tariff barriers, is present in most trade deals of the last generation.

In Asia, the TPP was surely the most advanced initiative in this sense. All the main articles pointed to an expansion of individual rights and a limitation of the capacity of states to exercise their sovereignty in economic matters. Moreover, all the key provisions were aimed protect economic rights from the intervention of the state.

China, since the reform era, has promoted its own unique form of "market", which political economists have defined as "State Capitalism" or "Sino-Capitalism". From our theoretical perspective, the crucial feature of the Chinese State Capitalism is its coherence with the pluralist vision of the international order preferred by China. The Chinese embracing of capitalism is instrumental and selective. Since the reform era, China has clearly accepted the need to integrate itself into the global economy and to progressively introduce elements of economic freedom and competition in its domestic system. Nevertheless, for different reasons, the Chinese embracing of capitalism remains uneven and partial. Firstly, as widely recognized in the literature on the subject, since the Deng era the Chinese leadership has promoted capitalist methods because they appeared to be the most useful instrument by which to achieve the key political objective of economic modernization and development. In other words, capitalist practices were functional for achieving wealth and power, not for the creation of an open society (Schell and Delury 2013).

Secondly, China has always considered the promotion of capitalism as an aim and not as an end. The liberalization of the economy is fundamentally limit by the ultimate political aim of the Communist Party of China (CPC), namely the maintenance of the Leninist political system and the monopoly of power. This entails the rejection of the solidarist features associated with advancing capitalist governance, such as regulations behind the borders and non-tariff barriers, which are considered as an attempt to interfere in China's sovereignty. On the contrary, the evolution of the Chinese model has been deeply influenced by the concept of "grasping the big, letting go the small" (*zhua da fang xiao*), namely the idea of privatizing small public companies, while retaining the control of large enterprises, that are considered essential economic and political instruments, domestically as well as in terms of foreign policy (Eaton 2015).

As pointed out by economists such as Huang, the private sector has been the real protagonist of the Chinese economic miracle, in terms of productivity (Huang 2008). Nevertheless, the CPC has theorized the necessity to maintain the control of the "commanding heights" of the economic system. Not because it is assumed that state control or public ownership is considered better in terms of social justice or production. The decision to maintain or even strengthen the control of the state and the Party over key sectors of the economy, such as finance and banking, and most heavy industries, stems from the idea that the economic system should remain an instrument controlled by the state, and should be used to pursue the national interests (Hsueh 2016).

From this perspective, the Chinese form of capitalism does not entail a retreat from state control and state sovereignty. The Chinese model of economic development is not centred on the necessity to protect the rights of the individual, but rather on allowing the country to find its own pattern of development and economic power, as a sovereign political community. Ultimately, this idea is coherent with the pluralist-sovereignist ideas which China has been promoting about the global and regional order. This understanding of "market" is crucial for analysing the way in which China has been promoting its regionalist blueprint. AIIB, BRI and RCEP are in fact deeply influenced by the idea that politics can remain in control of economic dynamics.

The theoretical framework presented in this chapter will allow us to analyze China's regional initiative from a unique point of view. We will look at how every regional initiative involves a specific effort to contest and reform the current regional order, while promoting China's interests and principles. Before this, in Chapter 2, we will introduce the fundamental ideation pillars of the narrative that helped to conceptualize and legitimize the Chinese challenge to the current regional order. China's attempt to reshape the regional (and global) order stems from a long process of intellectual and political elaboration. As we will see in the following chapter, the current Chinese leadership has based its blueprint for regional order on a mix of post-colonial nationalism and neo-Confucianism. These ideas represent the most relevant ideational resources deployed by Beijing to advance its alternative to the contemporary Western-led international order.

Bibliography

Acharya, Amitav. 2011. *Whose Ideas Matter? Agency and Power in Asian Regionalism*. Ithaca, NY: Cornell University Press.

Allison, Graham T. 2017. *Destined for War: Can America and China Escape Thucydides's Trap?* Boston, MA: Houghton Mifflin Harcourt.

ASEAN. 2016. "Treaty of Amity and Cooperation in South East Asia." Available at http://asean.org/treaty-amity-cooperation-southeast-asia-indonesia-24-february-1976/. Accessed 27 October 2017.

Beeson, Mark. 2006. "American Hegemony and Regionalism: The Rise of East Asia and the End of the Asia-Pacific." *Geopolitics* 114 (3): 541–560.

Bowles, Paul. 2002. "Asia's Post-crisis Regionalism: Bringing the State Back in Keeping the United States Out." *Review of International Political Economy* 92 (2): 244–270.

Brenner, Neil. 1998. "Between Fixity and Motion: Accumulation, Territorial Organization and the Historical Geography of Spatial Scales." *Environment and Planning D-Society and Space* 16 (4): 459–481.

Bull, Hedley. 1977. *The Anarchical Society: A Study of Order in World Politics*. London: Macmillan.

Bull, Hedley, and Adam Watson. 1984. "Conclusion." In *The Expansion of International Society*, edited by Hedley Bull and Adam Watson, 425–435. Oxford: Oxford University Press.

Bull, Hedley, and Adam Watson, eds. 1984. *The Expansion of International Society*. Oxford: Oxford University Press.

Buzan, Barry. 2004. *From International to World Society? English School Theory and the Social Structure of Globalisation*. Cambridge: Cambridge University Press.

Buzan, Barry. 2010. "China in International Society: Is "Peaceful Rise" Possible?" *The Chinese Journal of International Politics* 3 (1): 5–36.

Buzan, Barry. 2014. *An Introduction to the English School of International Relations: The Societal Approach*. Cambridge: Polity.

Buzan, Barry, and George Lawson. 2015. *The Great Transformation. The Global Transformation: History, Modernity and the Making of International Relations*. Cambridge: Cambridge University Press.

Buzan, Barry, and Yongjin Zhang, eds. 2014a. *Contesting International Society in Asia*. Cambridge: Cambridge University Press.

Buzan, Barry, and Yongjin Zhang. 2014b. "Introduction: Interrogating Regional International Society in East Asia." In *Contesting International Society in East Asia*, edited by Barry Buzan and Yogjin Zhang, 1–29. Cambridge: Cambridge University Press.

Costa-Buranelli, Filippo. 2015. "'Do You Know What I Mean?' 'Not Exactly': English School, Global International Society and the Polysemy of Institutions." *Global Discourse* 5 (3): 499–514.

Eaton, Sarah. 2015. *The Advance of the State in Contemporary China: State-Market Relations in the Reform Era*. Cambridge: Cambridge University Press.

Fairbank, John K. 1942. "Tributary Trade and China's Relations with the West." *The Far Eastern Quarterly* 1 (2): 129–149.

Foot, Rosemary. 2011. "The Responsibility to Protect (R2P) and Its Evolution: Beijing's Influence on Norm Creation in Humanitarian Areas." *St Antony's International Review* 6 (2): 47–66.

Friedberg, Aaron L. 1993. "Ripe for Rivalry: Prospects for Peace in a Multipolar Asia." *International Security* 18 (3): 5–33.

Gilpin, Robert G. 1984. "The Richness of the Tradition of Political Realism." *International Organization* 38 (2): 287–304.

Goh, Evelyn. 2013. *The Struggle for Order: Hegemony, Hierarchy, and Transition in Post-Cold War East Asia*. Oxford: Oxford University Press.

Goh, Evelyn. 2014. "East Asia as Regional International Society: The Problem of Great Power Management." In *Contesting International Society in East Asia*, edited by Barry Buzan and Yogjin Zhang, 167–187. Cambridge: Cambridge University Press.

Hall, Peter A., and David Soskice, eds. 2001. *Varieties of Capitalism. The Institutional Foundation of Comparative Advantage*. Oxford: Oxford University Press.

Hobson, John M. 2012. *The Eurocentric Conception of World Politics: Western International Theory, 1760–2010*. Cambridge: Cambridge University Press.

Hsueh, Roselyn. 2016. "State Capitalism, Chinese-Style: Strategic Value of Sectors, Sectoral Characteristics, and Globalization." *Governance* 29 (1): 85–101.

Huang, Yasheng. 2008. *Capitalism with Chinese Characteristics: Entrepreneurship and the State*. Cambridge: Cambridge University Press.

Hurrell, Andrew. 2007. *On Global Order: Power, Values, and the Constitution of International Society*. Oxford: Oxford University Press.
Ikenberry, G. John. 2008. "The Rise of China: Power, Institutions, and the Western Order." In *China's Ascent: Power, Security, and the Future of International Politics*, edited by Robert S. Ross and Zhu Feng, 89–114. Ithaca, NY: Cornell University Press.
Johnston, Alastair Iain. 2008. *Social States: China in International Institutions, 1980–2000*. Princeton: Princeton University Press.
Kang, David C. 2008. *China Rising: Peace, Power, and Order in East Asia*. New York: Columbia University Press.
Kang, David C. 2010. *East Asia before the West: Five Centuries of Trade and Tribute*. New York: Columbia University Press.
Kirshner, Jonathan. 2010. "The Tragedy of Offensive Realism: Classical Realism and the Rise of China." *European Journal of International Relations* 18 (3): 53–75.
Linklater, Andrew. 1998. *The Transformation of Political Community: Ethical Foundations of the Post-Westphalian Era*. Chapel Hill, NC: University of South Carolina Press.
Loke, Beverley. 2016. "Unpacking the Politics of Great Power Responsibility: Nationalist and Maoist China in International Order-Building." *European Journal of International Relations* 22 (4): 847–871.
Mearsheimer, John J. 2010. "The Gathering Storm: China's Challenge to US Power in Asia." *The Chinese Journal of International Politics* 3 (4): 381–396.
Narine, Shaun. 2004. "State Sovereignty, Political Legitimacy and Regional Institutionalism in the Asia-Pacific." *The Pacific Review* 17 (3): 423–450.
Narine, Shaun. 2006. "The English School and ASEAN." *The Pacific Review* 19 (2): 199–218.
Naughton, Barry, and Kellee S. Tsai, eds. 2015. *State Capitalism, Institutional Adaptation, and the Chinese Miracle*. Cambridge: Cambridge University Press.
Permanent Mission of the PRC to the UN. 2009, July 24. "Statement by Ambassador Liu Zhenmin at the Plenary Session of the General Assembly on the Question of 'Responsibility to Protect'." Available at http://www.china-un.org/eng/lhghyywj/smhwj/2009/t575682.htm.
Schell, Oliver, and John Delury. 2013. *Wealth and Power: China's Long March to the Twenty-First Century*. London: Random House.
Söderbaum, Fredrick. 2014. "Theories of Regionalism." In *The Routledge Handbook of Asian Regionalism*, edited by Mark Beeson and Richard Subbs, 11–21. London: Routledge.
Stivachtis, Yannis A. 2015. "Interrogating Regional International Societies, Questioning the Global International Society." *Global Discourse* 5 (3): 327–340.

Stivachtis, Yannis A., and Mark Webber. 2015. "Regional International Society in a Post-enlargement Europe. Europe After Enlargement." *Journal of European Integration* 33 (2): 101–116.

Suzuki, Shogo. 2014. "Europe at the Periphery of the Japanese World Order." In *International Orders in the Early Modern World*, edited by Shogo Suzuki, Yongjin Zhang, and Joel Quirk, 76–93. London: Routledge.

Vogel, Ezra F. 2011. *Deng Xiaoping and the Transformation of China*. Cambridge, MA: Harvard University Press.

Watson, Adam. 1992. *The Evolution of International Society: A Comparative Historical Analysis Reissue with a New Introduction by Barry Buzan and Richard Little*. London: Routledge.

Weede, Erich. 2010. "The Capitalist Peace and the Rise of China: Establishing Global Harmony by Economic Interdependence." *International Interactions* 36 (2): 206–213.

Zhang, Xiaoming. 2011. "China in the Conception of International Society: The English School's Engagements with China." *Review of International Studies* 37 (2): 763–786.

Zhang, Yongjin. 2014. "Curious and Exotic Encounters: Europeans as Supplicants in the Chinese Imperium, 1514–1793." In *International Orders in the Early Modern World*, edited by Shogo Suzuki, Yongjin Zhang, and Joel Quirk, 55–75. London: Routledge.

Zhang, Yongjin. 2015. "Regional International Society in East Asia? A Critical Investigation." *Global Discourse* 5 (3): 360–373.

Zhang, Yongjin. 2016. "China and Liberal Hierarchies in Global International Society: Power and Negotiation for Normative Change." *International Affairs* 92 (4): 795–816.

Zhang, Yongjin, and Barry Buzan. 2012. "The Tributary System as International Society in Theory and Practice." *Chinese Journal of International Politics* 5 (1): 3–36.

CHAPTER 2

The Origin of China's Ideational Narratives

Abstract This chapter presents the ideational pillars shaping China's legitimation process concerning major initiatives within regional and global governance. It suggests the idea that the origin, the normative content, and the institutional structures of the initiatives and organizations recently established by China at the regional and global level are vigorously influenced with the way the CCP legitimizes its own ideational narratives in global politics. While arguing so, the chapter analyses two major ideational narratives, post-colonial nationalism and neo-Confucianism. The chapter also examines major political frames through which the Xi Jinping administration is building its legitimacy and strategy while reshaping China's foreign policy: the China Dream, a new type of international relations and a new type of international institutions.

Keywords Ideational narratives · Post-colonialism · Neo-Confucianism China Dream · A new type of international relations · A new type of international institutions

Introduction

There is a widespread international debate on the Chinese vision of the global order. Debate in the West, and particularly in the US, has tended to frame Beijing's growing authority in international affairs either as a hegemonic transition or as a result of a growing

M. Dian and S. Menegazzi, *New Regional Initiatives in China's Foreign Policy*, https://doi.org/10.1007/978-3-319-75505-2_2

economic interdependence and institutionalization in global governance. With China's rejuvenation, the debate has changed once again, focusing on what Chinese leaders and policymakers claim to be the most important priorities for strengthening China's international influence. This chapter examines the ideational pillars shaping China's legitimization process concerning major initiatives within regional and global governance. It considers China's foreign policy ideational strategies as being deeply influenced by the Westphalian orientation towards major narratives of international politics and, as such, strongly intertwined with certain pluralist elements, as exemplified by the theoretical tradition of the English School literature in international relations theorizing, i.e., sovereignty, self-determination and ideological differences among countries.

China's ideational narratives present a fundamental challenge to understanding Beijing's behaviour in international politics, as well as the intentions of the Chinese leadership's *vis-à-vis* foreign policy and diplomatic practices. Ideas, ideological narratives and normative components are today deemed to be essential for our understanding of China's role in the international environment, as they shape and affect China's behaviour within regional and global governance. Early February 2017 saw discussions on the importance of possessing a global vision for China's international politics. It was the moment when the Chinese President, Xi Jinping, stressed for the very first time the country's new approach towards international relations, the "two guides" policy (两个引导 *liang ge yindao*), namely the new world order and international security. Citing Xi's words, it is possible to understand how China's willingness to reform the international system from within is growing closer to Chinese ideas and practices, but especially in parallel with the intent to go beyond a Western-dominated world order:

> China is qualified to be a leader. The glorious history of the Chinese nation for five thousand years, the struggle of the Chinese Communist Party in the past ninety-five years, the miracle of the thirty-eight years of reforms and opening-up, have been declared to the world as undeniable facts. We are qualified to be able to become the leaders of a new international order and of international security. (Chinese Cadre Learning Network 2017)

In this chapter, we suggest that the origin, the normative content and the institutional structure of the initiatives and organizations led by China in regional and global politics—and which will be further analysed within the book (i.e., the BRI, the AIIB and the RCEP)—are strongly connected to the way the CCP legitimizes its own ideational narrative in global politics. This is particularly true once we analyse China's legacy through ideational concepts and political narratives, whether post-colonial nationalism or through the rise of neo-Confucianism. In the last decade, China strongly committed itself to depicting an image of a country capable of developing an alternative model to Western standards, norms and practices in the international environment. Since many recently established projects have triggered a new interest among scholars, we believe it is particularly useful to unravel the precise ideational origins behind the different initiatives. A further aim of the chapter is to discuss the extent to which new concepts promoted by the Fifth Generation of Leaders (i.e., concepts such as the China Dream, a New Type of Great Power Relations, and a New Type of International Institutions) are capable of shaping and influencing the way in which China constructs and maintains its leadership role within new initiatives at regional and global levels.

Examining the ideational narratives of China's international behaviour in this way also necessitates a shift in international political thinking from the Hobbesian perspective, in which China's role in world politics is trapped by great power politics conceiving its rise exclusively as something to inhibit or deflect (Dian 2017). Instead, we need to analyse China's international behaviour as the result of different ideational narratives—some of which are rooted in its past and previous experiences, whereas others are mostly related to contemporary international dynamics. Considering ideas and political narratives as a central element of Chinese foreign policy provides us with a starting point for analysing several key initiatives in which China is becoming a prominent leader regionally and globally, and for examining how they are affecting existing institutions and practices. This, we argue, provides unambiguous evidence for thinking about China as a proactive player of the global order, rather than a simple bystander. As we will see throughout the book, the assumption does not mean as many have argued, that China's foreign policy is today more aggressive or, that the Chinese rise is threatening the future of the global order. Undoubtedly, since Xi Jinping came to power in November 2012, China's foreign policy guidelines underwent a sudden change of course. For instance, in October 2013, when declaring the main priorities for the People's Republic of China (PRC) foreign policy during his term in office, Xi did not talk about Deng Xiaoping's foreign policy mantra, 韬光养晦 (*tao guang yang hui*—hiding one's capabilities and biding one's time). Rather, he emphasized the idea of 奋发有为 (*fenfa you wei*—striving for achievements) (2016). Nevertheless, China's current vision of the global order has been presented by its rise, coupled with a relative consciousness about a certain decline of the West. As such, it is precisely this global power shift that is generating greater opportunities for change, together with more opportunities for Chinese interests and objectives to grow, which most likely, seem to be in line with leaders' expectations (Breslin and Menegazzi 2017).

Post-colonial Nationalism and Neo-Confucianism

Theoretical narratives which see international politics as a reflection of people's ideas about the world are today broadly accepted in the IR discipline. This is because approaches considering material interests as the only forces shaping people or the actions and behaviour of states in the world cannot fully provide us with an exhaustive explanation of political reality. For instance, they often tend to omit the importance of acknowledging the existence of different visions of world order. This, according to Marchetti, explains the dichotomy at play in terms of master frames created today between Western powers and non-Western countries. While Western powers tend to have a universalistic approach to global governance, countries like Russia or China believe instead that context matters, and they therefore sustain the idea that in international politics each country should preserve its own political regime as well as the uniqueness of its political sovereignty (Marchetti 2017).

The concept of post-colonial nationalism stands as an important "idea" in the contemporary Chinese foreign policy narrative. On many occasions, it can be considered as the ideational foundation pushing Chinese leaders to discuss and spread major political ideas both within and outside China. For instance, it is not unusual to hear Chinese politicians referring to strict adherence to the Five Principles of Peaceful Co-existence, which often remain at the centre of the Chinese proposals, in terms of regional and global governance. This happened on the occasion of the commemorative ceremony marking the 60th anniversary of the ratification of the "Five Principles of the Peaceful Coexistence":

> These principles offer a powerful intellectual tool for developing countries to uphold their sovereignty and independence, and they have thus

> become a rallying call for enhancing solidarity, cooperation and strength among them. These principles have deepened the mutual understanding and trust among developing countries, boosted South-South cooperation and also contributed to the improvement of North-South relations. The Five Principles of Peaceful Coexistence have played a positive role in building a more equitable and rational international political and economic order. Rejecting the law of the jungle by which the strong bullies the weak, the Five Principles of Peaceful Coexistence strengthened the movement against imperialism and colonialism that eventually brought colonialism to an end. (China.org 2014)

The embracing of the five principles denotes the enduring post-colonial identity of the Chinese state. China overcame colonialism and imperialism, and emerged from the Century of Humiliation with the need to protect its independence, sovereignty and self-determination as a main priority. This does not imply the necessity to isolate China from the global order. On the contrary, there are many reasons for China to participate in it. As noted by Shaun Breslin, from the end of the Cold War, China successfully integrated itself into the vast array of international politics through a series of multilateral initiatives, including those undertaken with Brazil, Russia, India, China and South Africa (BRICS) countries; the creation of the Shanghai Cooperation Organization (SCO); and the establishment of political fora such as the China–Caribbean Economy and Trade Cooperation Forum (CCETCF) up to its recent and growing involvement as a member of the G20 (Breslin 2015).

Post-colonial nationalism has led China to develop an exceptionalist narrative about its role in global politics, one that does not posit the Chinese surge as a threat to the East Asian region and the entire world. At the same time, it has helped China to build a narrative willing to support South-South relations in global governance, as opposed to the once totally Western-led world order. As a result, a rising China is described as entirely beneficial to its neighbours and its partners. Furthermore, China is presented as capable of escaping the "Thucydides's trap" or the dangers related to power transition, because of its identity as a country that suffered colonialism. Within such a discourse, China's behaviour is not considered to be driven by hegemonic concerns. China's regional strategic growing role in South East Asia is presented as both a threat and an opportunity, and the balance of such a perception has oscillated along a spectrum over the last decade. Economically, Southeast Asian businesses and elites have benefited from China's growing presence in the region, but politically, many states in South East Asia fear the growing competition that it might escalate between Washington and Beijing. Nevertheless, China has three main concerns that it wants to guarantee in the region, and these are sovereignty, territorial integrity and national security (Goh 2015). From this point of view, its strategic political imperative in the region is not driven by great power politics dynamics, but rather, by the intent to preserve the integrity of the identity of the Chinese state.

The ideological narrative and the political rationale behind such a perspective is that China's ascent is not aimed at increasing hegemonic competition, nor does it totally disrupt the international order. Rather, China's top priority is its foreign policy practices, i.e., domestic development and the construction of win-win relations with its neighbourhood and other major powers. Peter J. Katzenstein affirmed that in order to understand the rise of China, we should combine three lenses of categories for explanation, i.e., rupture, return and recombination, together with the cultural, economic and security dimensions. *Rupture*, in the sense that China's ascent provoked an unprecedented change transforming the East Asian region and the entire world economy. *Return*, as China is today the epicentre of economic and political transformation as in fact, it has always been (Century of National Humiliation excluded). *Recombination*, as China's place in world affairs is the result of "the recombination of old and new patterns and components" of the international system within which Western-centred and Eurocentric views now coexist with Chinese perspectives and the process of Sinicization (Katzestein 2012). From here however, emerges the necessity to link China's rejuvenation narrative with its postcolonial experience and consequent ideas about its visions of world order and major foreign policy interests, such as sovereignty or non-interference. This brings us back to the fact that when applied to China, narratives such as postcolonial nationalism cannot ignore the suffering left by the wounds of the "Century of National Humiliation", which remains today as a useful way to explain for instance China's reluctance to supranational rules in the framework of global governance practices. In the same way, Florini emphasizes the necessity to acknowledge "the days when Western, and particularly American, intellectuals and policymakers could set the terms for the debates over IR and the management of global issues are over" (Florini 2011, p. 32). In this sense, it is not simply a matter of incorporating Chinese ideas and narratives into global policymaking, but the fact that as a result of China's tsunami in world affairs, previous theories and practices of international politics lost their credibility without including a Chinese perspective. Since the early 1980s, Chinese scholars learned, translated and used Western IR theories for the study of international politics. Nevertheless, as explained by Qin Yaqin, Professor at China Foreign Affairs University, concerns were raised by scholars about two major issues: first, whether it is acceptable to use exclusively Western theories in order to explain non-Western practices in international politics, and second, whether we should include a cultural perspective in international relations theories, going beyond universalistic approaches so far proposed by American scholars (Qin 2015).

To some extent, it was precisely the suffering and long periods of humiliating domination by Western powers that gave Chinese leaders, policymakers and public intellectuals the strength to reassure China of its dominant international role, together with the need to ensure non-Western concepts and political narratives to be included.

In a similar vein, to re-think the role of China within the new and increasingly multipolar global order, the Chinese leadership has resorted to neo-Confucian concepts and beliefs. In the last two decades, Confucian ideas have become intellectual resources providing solutions to the dilemma of how to think and legitimize a new role for China in the twenty-first century. Since Xi Jinping took office in October 2012, in particular, the CCP revived the Confucian tradition in an unprecedented way, compared with his predecessors. Remarkably, the speech Xi gave at the Commemoration of the 2565th Anniversary of Confucius' birth in 2014, affirmed the intention to uphold Confucian values as fundamental elements of Chinese contemporary politics and society:

> The ideology and culture of today's China is also the continuation and sublimation of traditional Chinese ideology and culture. To understand present-day China, to know the present-day Chinese, one must delve into the cultural bloodline of China, and accurately appreciate the cultural soil that nourishes the Chinese people…Studying Confucius and Confucianism is an important approach to understanding the national characteristics of the Chinese as well as the historical roots of the spiritual world of the present-day Chinese. (China-US Focus 2014)

Within such a perspective, the Confucian tradition becomes a fundamental element for understanding how leaders in Beijing construct China's political narrative as being rooted in its ancient and historical past.

The approach does not imply the abandonment of Marxism: rather, it implies a combination of the two that allows China to distinguish itself as a country faithful to its political identity while being aware of the cultural tradition of its people:

> Members of the Communist Party of China are Marxists, who uphold the scientific theories of Marxism, and adhere to and develop socialism with Chinese characteristics. But Chinese communists are neither historical nihilists, nor cultural nihilists. We always believe that the basic principles of Marxism must be closely married to the concrete reality of China, and that we should approach traditional native culture and cultures of all countries in a scientific manner, and arm ourselves with all outstanding cultural achievements humanity has created. (China-US Focus 2014).

He explains the necessity to distinguish between different types of Confucian traditions in China. What He defines as "Political Confucianism" is the doctrine affecting the most ideas and political narratives used by Xi Jinping and policymakers at the global level. The main assumption is that such a narrative "is aimed at revitalizing Confucianism and reconstructing the politics of the kingly way (王道 *wangdao*) in the modern global context" (Li 2015: 82). Unsurprisingly, the concept is used as a discourse juxtaposed with Western models and ideas in which the intent is to highlight how the Western experience of development should be considered as decadent in today's world, and therefore, as harmful to China. He further maintains that the revival of Confucianism in China is due to other factors, such as Confucian ethic having become a fundamental motivation for the economic miracle of the Asian society. Another reason is the support of the Party for traditional concepts such as socialism with Chinese characteristics. Traditions, in this sense, can reinforce propaganda slogans sustained by leaders about their importance for contemporary China. Furthermore, 新儒家 (*xin rujia*)—literally New Confucianism—is an intellectual as well as a cultural phenomenon strengthening the awareness of the Chinese people and their role in the world. China's role and its new developmental path at the international level is profoundly affected by its "exceptionalism", in which neither the Soviet model nor the Western idea of development could ever stand as real examples for China. Rather, as sustained by CCP leaders, China should look at its own way of development, and more importantly, operate in line with its ancient historical tradition (Zhang 2017). To some extent, the attempt to revive Confucianism stands in contrast with the official Marxist discourse embraced by Chinese leaders since Mao's time. Confucianism and Marxism are two conflicting ideologies that do not share many ideological principles or philosophical assumptions. Yet, it is a fact that given the Party's interests, today the two narratives are used in parallel by Chinese leaders to guarantee the sustainability of political agendas and to strengthen popular consensus. Furthermore, through Confucianism, the Party's legacy in foreign policy practices is guaranteed by emphasizing Confucius' teachings and pacifist values, i.e., peace and harmony, thus reducing China's international reputation as a rising hegemon (Liu 2014).

A Dream for China

Narratives such as post-colonialism and New Confucianism are rooted in China's selective appropriation of ideas originating in the Chinese past and its historical experiences. More recently however, the Chinese leadership started to make constant use of new political concepts and ideas, in order to reinforce China's image at the international level. Among them, it is probably the concept of the *China Dream* that has drawn the greatest worldwide attention. Ideated under the Xi Jinping administration, the concept is deeply intertwined with the dialectic between humiliation and rejuvenation, as well as being influenced by the idea of historical righteousness and historical determinism inherited by the Marxist–Leninist ideology. According to CASS professor Tingyang Zhao, the concept of the China dream is profoundly rooted in China's need to provide a political narrative, which resulted from its past and was interlinked with the concept of the *tianxia* system.[1] The necessity to construct what could be defined at all costs as an "ideal type narrative" for the Chinese civilization in the twenty-first century stands, according to Zhao, as the consequence of two intertwined dynamics suffered by China at the end of the twenty-first century: the fact is that at that time China was a peaceful power lacking any sort of imperialism, thus the constant race made by China to achieve the same level of modernization as foreign countries did in the West. However, "because China's dream of modernization is essentially westernization, it is

[1]The tianxia system is translated from Chinese into English as 'all-under-heaven'. See Tingyang Zhao (2006).

therefore not a dream of China, or a dream of Chineseness, yet it remains the only way for China to survive. Even more challenging, westernization is the devaluation of Chinese traditions and the systematic transformation of China into a nation dependent on the Western system and game" (Zhao 2014). Within such a perspective, the concept of the China Dream advanced by Xi Jinping is the result of China's rejuvenation into the international system, depicting the image of a country free from imperialism and thus conscious instead of its post-colonial identity. At the same time, the Chinese Dream, according to Chinese scholars, is to work to enrich the development of Marxism and strengthen socialist modernization, which appears very different from the American dream (Liao 2016a, b). At present, it is thus deemed to be essential to advocate a precise image of China and the development of its political theories and disciplines, at home and abroad (Zhang 2015).

When initially proposed, the concept of the China Dream (中国梦 *Zhongguo meng*) seemed, at a glance, mostly oriented toward China's domestic level, as a political narrative stressing the legitimacy of both the party and the regime, while being opposed to Western values based on concepts such as the middle class, individualism and democracy. It is not surprising, then, how the idea of a China Dream engendered some antipathy in the West. The concept has been charged with increasing nationalism: it has exacerbated historical victimhood among the population, and tightened centralization (i.e., it gives more power to the party than to the people). To some, Xi's narrative is nothing new in the Chinese political discourse, but its peculiarity is precisely about his methodology: consolidating power through the use of traditional values (Xian 2016).

But, at the same time, the Chinese Dream exemplified important directives regarding Chinese foreign policy. First and foremost, it is a sign that Deng Xiaoping's *tao guang yang hui* approach to international politics has been replaced. Secondly, it is a narrative employed by political leaders to ensure China's peaceful development strategy abroad. Finally, the idea of China Dream is part of a narrative constructed by the Xi Jinping administration in order to build China's image at the international level as a "normative power", whose foreign policy initiatives and interests are driven by the intent to build a Sino-centric world order and Chinese rules for global governance.

Among Western academics, William Callahan, devoted particular attention in his work since the generation, through the elaboration and up to the transformation of the political narrative concerning the China Dream.

Since the concept was initially proposed when Xi Jinping took office as the general secretary of the CCP in 2012, Callahan analysed the leadership's discourse, public intellectual reactions, and the implications the narrative attained at the international level, in light of an identity politics perspective. For Callahan, two main consideration stand out regarding the political discourse proposed by the Fifth Generation's Leader. First, the China Dream is part of a narrative that appears to contrast with what policymakers in China, affirmed since the concept was initially proposed. First, the China Dream narrative is neither inclusive nor egalitarian, contrary to Xi Jinping's claims. Furthermore, the narrative, "does not promote liberal reform, it employs the illiberal ideas/identities of socialism and Chinese civilization to charts China's future" (Callahan 2016). Second, is the extent to which the idea of the China Dream explains China's role in world affairs as a counter-hegemon power *vis-à-vis* the US. Indeed, Xi's Dream is not merely an explanation of the "great rejuvenation of the Chinese nations", but a narrative, eventually a strategy, which helps China how to think about itself as a great power in the twenty-first century (Callahan 2015). This is particularly evident if we consider that the China Dream now includes an Asia-Pacific Dream and a World Dream, bringing back a Sinocentric world order while locating the future of Asia directly in China's imperial past. According to Callaghan, the idea is "very traditional with a hierarchical view of domestic society and international society" (Callahan 2015, p. 4).

A New Type of International Relations

The China Dream narrative helped policymakers, elites as well as public intellectuals, to imagine and construct political ideas about China's role as a great power in the twenty-first century. The juxtaposition not only occurred in a state-level perspective, but also concerning the narrative in itself, i.e., comparing the China Dream with the American Dream. The critique of American hegemonism from a Neo-Confucian perspective is merged with the dialectic between humiliation-rejuvenation, while bringing in another central narrative for Chinese foreign policy, namely the promotion of "a new type of international relations" (新型国际关系 *xinxing guoji guanxi*). This concept is associated to the idea that China aims to achieve and promote greater democracy in international relations, without double standards, as affirmed by Xi Jinping (Xinhua 2014). This means, more practically, promoting cooperative and positive-sum games, win-win relations with other countries through the reform of global governance—yet better upholding the rights and interests of developing countries rather than primarily the interests of the West, as well as avoiding any kind of hegemonic behaviour while considering the interests of all countries involved. According to Micheal Swaine, the concept of building a "new type of international relations" draws from the previous concept "a new type of great powers relations" (新型大国关系 *xinxing daguo guanxi*). The difference between the two is that whereas the former is addressed to all types of inter-state relations, the latter deals exclusively with US–China relations (Swaine 2014). Broadly speaking, many scholars and analysts alike failed to pay excessive attention to the distinction between the two concepts. For instance, some believe the concept of "a new type of major power relations" should be applied to China's foreign policy indistinctively, whereas others believe it relates exclusively to China's relationship with the US.

Within such a perspective, and particularly considering international relations theorizing to understand the concept, some IR scholars someone believe it should be framed more practically into the realism and neo-realism debates. For instance, according to Joseph Y.S. Cheng, despite Beijing politics still following the line of Marxism–Leninism, realist thinking in fact prevails in the way Chinese policymakers think and behave about international politics (Chang 2016). Not only is the China–US relationship a top priority in Chinese foreign policy: great power politics dynamics, strategic and security issues, as well as the future of global power configuration, represent a main priority for China's leaders and the Xi Jinping administration. From a rather different perspective, Su Hao, highlights how the substitution of the word "powers" for "countries" was an essential manoeuvre for understanding China's approach to international politics:

> Regarding this concept, if we want to translate it from Chinese into English, we should translate it a "New Type of Major Countries Relations", not "great power relations" because originally, the so-called powers means (hard) power orientation in international politics, which means the use of power to projects the use of force to the other side, with a certain impact on the others, and this is not a Chinese mean, so this is the reason why we change this concept and the use of the words "major powers". A second implication with regards to this type of concept is that we want to change the logic to define the power relations among countries. (Su Hao, interview with author, Rome 2015)

The concept of a "new model of major power relationship" (新型大国关系 *xinxing daguo guanxi*) was initially proposed by Xi Jinping in 2012 when he visited the US—which means, before he took office as the general secretary of the CCP. Then in 2013, during his first official meeting with the American President Barack Obama in California, Xi Jinping delineated the major guidelines for China's foreign policy in relation to the US:

> China and the U.S. should blaze a new path different from that of conflicts and confrontation between great powers in history. Both sides agreed that we will build together a new type of relationship between great powers based on mutual respect, cooperation and win-win results for the benefit of the people of the two countries as well as of the world. The international community also expects for continuous improvement and development in China-US relations. A good cooperative relationship between China and the U.S. is conducive to world stability and peace. (Ministry of Foreign Affairs 2013)

American scholars such as David M. Lampton believe that the concept was formulated exclusively for the future of development of the Sino-American relationship. He was positive, however, about its global implications. Distancing himself from Mearsheimer's offensive realism to address the China–US issue, Lampton believed that by substituting mistrust and popular anxiety with common benefits and cooperation, as suggested by China, the two countries might avoid high levels of confrontation and conflict, benefiting ongoing dynamics global politics at large (Lampton 2013). More recently, however, official discourses in which the concept has been used also included China's relations with other countries, most probably Russia, but also Japan.

When in 2015 the compilation of Xi Jinping's political theories *The Governance of China* was published, the translated formula had been transformed into a "New Model of Major-Country Relations" and attention had been directed further toward Russia, the US and Europe. Although China welcomes a G2 scenario in the future, it seems that it is still pushing forward the idea of a multipolar rather than a bipolar world order. Xi Jinping's idea of building a new type of international relations represents the core of China's foreign policy narrative and diplomatic practices. The official discourse has been widely presented to domestic and foreign audiences and the idea has already achieved important theoretical and practical implications (Pan 2016). In this regard, the discourse pronounced by Wang Yi at the China Development Forum in 2015 was an essential moment for understanding the future of China and its political narrative. In the words of the Chinese Minister of Foreign Affairs, the programme for a "new type of international relations" for China is clear: to build win-win cooperation at the core of the international relations system politically, economically, culturally and, with a focus on security issues (Ministry of Foreign Affairs 2016).

Politically, Chinese leaders evince the view that China needs to build alliances at the international level, but avoiding hegemonic behaviour. In this sense, although the relationship with the US remains a top priority, so it is with Russia, the EU, Africa and the Latin American countries. Economically, China intends to provide finance and infrastructure building along the Silk Road through new institutions and financial activities, prime among which are the AIIB and the Silk Road Fund. As for security issues, China clearly recognizes the importance of existing multilateral institutions, particularly the United Nations (UN). At the same time, it is promoting China-led multilateral initiatives, such as the SCO, while increasingly it upholds the idea of discussing political issues outside official channels, i.e., through the implementation of "Track 2" dialogues with ASEAN countries. Understanding the narrative adopted by the Xi Jinping administration, as well as the management of international relations, is essential for our understanding of China's ideas about the future of world order.

After more than three decades of economic transformation, China attained an unprecedented level of trust among other countries regarding global governance, particularly by developing nations, concerning economic, political, social, environmental, foreign policy and security issues. Over the next 10 years, the political and economic strategies China will pursue at the international level will be the key not only to China's economic development but to that of many other countries worldwide. As the BRI recently demonstrated, China intends to promote its own model of development going beyond emerging economies environments and developing realities, as for instance, through the significant programme of infrastructure building expected to be developed all along the Eurasian region. The key at stake for China at this moment is precisely the ability to find the right balance between a political narrative pushing forward Chinese interests in international affairs, as was done it in the past, or whether the willingness to push forward a more just and egalitarian international order will be an achievable outcome in the years ahead.

A New Model of Global Governance

Xi and other leaders employed Confucian ideas of harmony, mutual benefit, and inclusiveness, to describe the new Chinese initiatives in the field of regional economic governance and international cooperation. Xi himself has stated that the "One Belt One Road initiative inherits the normative ideals of peace, friendship, goodwill and coexistence, and harmonious development" that characterized China's imperial foreign policies and the Confucian ethic. China's promotion of "a new type of international institutions" and more broadly a deep engagement with the international order, serves the national interest in economic and political terms and facilitates the process of recognition of China's new status as a great power. AIIB, and RCEP are not presented as a substitute for the IMF and World Bank, nor as a first step towards the edification of a Chinese hegemony in Asia. On the contrary, they are tailored to protect the interests of developing countries, especially those in Asia. This testifies to the Chinese capacity to understand the needs of the developing world and the wish of the developing countries to protect their sovereignty and self-determination from the intrusiveness of the Western-led international institutions.

This approach positively resonates in the Asian region, where many states are critical of the Western, and, in particular, the American will to impose Western norms and standards. Ultimately, a call for a new order and new institutions based on tolerance, win-win relations and non-discrimination has found positive responses in the region. On the other hand, these concepts are also associated with a Sino-centric and hierarchical vision of the region and the world, and with a certain paternalism that might damage China's capacity to build a stable consensus on its initiatives. Within such a framework, what is really at stake is to comprehend what type of global order China is really thinking of for the years ahead. As the previous chapter exemplified, analysing the Chinese rise in the light of the English School perspective allowed us to go beyond traditional IR theorizing, and indeed beyond the realist and liberalist accounts of international politics, whose explanations about China's establishment of regional initiatives such as the AIIB or the RCEP only partially provide exhaustive explanations of Beijing's changing role *vis-à-vis* the regional and the global order. Furthermore, the Chinese approach to global governance today presents significant differences with the past, one within which Beijing's leaders are trying to give to the international community a different image of China based on harmony, mutual benefit and inclusiveness. The speech by the Chinese President at the World Economic Forum in Davos in 2017 was enlightening for our understanding of China's vision of global governance and how to manage it:

> There was a time when China also had doubts about economic globalization, and was not sure whether it should join the World Trade Organization. But we came to the conclusion that integration into the global economy is a historical trend. To grow its economy, China must have the courage to swim in the vast ocean of the global market. If one is always afraid of bracing the storm and exploring the new world, he will sooner or later get drowned in the ocean. Therefore, China took a brave step to embrace the global market. We have had our fair share of choking in the water and encountered whirlpools and choppy waves, but we have learned how to swim in this process. It has proved to be a right strategic choice. (America CGTN 2017)

Xi's words allow us to comprehend how Chinese leaders intend their country to be an essential element of economic globalization and global economic governance. China's approach towards the international economic order appears different from the one it had in the past. For instance sixteen years ago, when it took it fifteen years to officially join the WTO as the 143th member country (China formally submitted its request to join the GATT in 1986). Notwithstanding China's enthusiasm to be part of many different Western-led organizations, such as WTO or the World Bank, dissatisfaction continued to grow within the same international financial institutions (IFIs) precisely because of the limits imposed on non-Western countries and latecomer economies. As noted by Rapkin and Strand, it was indeed the inertia but even more, the conservative tendencies of existing powers that contributed the most to the fact that East Asian economies started to perceive their role in international institutions as being fairly represented (Rapkin 2003).

During the last decade, China—today the second largest economy in the world—took the lead in advocating under-representation within existing IFIs. More practically, China's dissatisfaction has been guided by the delicate balance at play regarding a country's weight in the world economy, the size of quotas within a certain organization, and the respective number of votes. However, China went one step further, establishing its own IFIs through the collaboration of so-called emerging economies, i.e., with the BRICS. For instance, only five years ago no-one could have anticipated the UK entering into a newly established multilateral development bank almost entirely managed by developing countries (the AIIB). However, within the regional and global initiatives recently established by China, the normative components, as well the structure and the organizational form of these organizations, are what differentiates China most from its Western counterparts. Some Chinese scholars explained it as the need for China to build a new model of global governance. Ding Yifan, from the State Council Development Research Center, stressed that one of the reasons why China established the AIIB is because the new initiative represents a *new type of international financial institutions* (一个新型的国际金融机构 *yige xinxing de guoji jinrong jigou*).

In Ding's view, China has neither the capacity nor the desire to resemble the American hegemonic role regarding IFIs. Similarly, Beijing's intention with the establishment of the AIIB is not to replace the Asian Development Bank or the World Bank. Rather, China is trying to supplement the existing international monetary and financial system, to cater for the needs of Asia. Accordingly, existing IFIs have been unable to meet the standards of a world fast-changing economy. Emerging markets wanted the two major financial institutions to reform (IMF and WB), to improve their rights to speak, but so far, the two leading institutions have not failed to listen to the developing countries' requests for reform. As a reaction, we saw the establishment of the Silk Road Fund and the BRICS Development Bank, and the birth of the AIIB as a collective response from those who had been unheeded in global governance for a long time (Ding 2015).

Conclusion

Today, there is a widespread debate in the West on whether China's growing involvement in global economic governance will lead Beijing to challenge international norms and institutions, particularly following the establishment of initiatives such as BRI and AIIB, or China's growing involvement into the RCEP project. This chapter has examined the ideational resources, ideas and political frames through which the Xi Jinping administration is building its legitimacy and strategy in order to reshape Chinese foreign policy's initiatives at the regional and global level. The chapter has focused on two major intellectual narratives: postcolonialism and Neo-Confucianism, as well as three ideational resources deployed by the Xi Jinping administration, i.e., the China Dream, a new type of international relations, and a new type of international institutions. China has been simultaneously following political narratives that are particularly supportive of its post-colonial identity and ancient historical tradition, without abandoning the roots of its political ideology, that is, a clear feature of China's intention to support the selective appropriation of concepts generated within the Chinese "ideational" past. Indeed, ideologically, as well as officially, China remains a socialist country; but as the CCP no longer runs a market-planned economy, other ideational narratives have fulfilled the void left by Marxism (Ai 2009). This also allowed Beijing leaders to reinforce the discourse about a certain degree of solidarity between China and the developing countries with the result of reinforcing China's South-South cooperation strategy. As result, non-Western countries perceive China today not as a rising hegemon as it was for the US, but rather, as a valuable alternative to it, with the ability to have a profound impact on the global order, and in line with the interests of dissatisfied emerging powers.

China specialist Suisheng Zhao suggests that China does not appear to be interested to overtaking the US power, or to articulate completely distinctive values as to totally disrupt the global order. Instead, through a Sino-centric, hierarchical view of the world order, while embracing Westphalian principles of sovereignty and non-intervention, China intends to change its position *within* the order, to increase its voice and weight into international institutions, while adjusting some rules and norms of behaviour once established exclusively by Western powers (Zhao 2016). In this light, and as exemplified in the previous chapter, the English School perspective is enlightening regarding some aspects of the pluralist order as the ideal type of international order advanced by China in the twenty-first century—most likely, the idea that each state is sovereign in its own territory, as well as the need to recognize ideological differences among states.

Since Xi Jinping took office in 2012, the administration has paid increasing attention to employing political narratives and ideational resources legitimizing newly establishing projects as essential alternatives to the contemporary Western-led international order. From this perspective, as explained by Peter Ferdinand, Xi Jinping launched a number of key foreign policy initiatives in order to make an active contribution to international governance (Ferdinand 2016). More specifically, the China dream campaign will be nothing more than the moral rationale aimed at supporting the economic dimensions and geopolitical implications of China's policy innovations, as "the China dream is one of surpassing… the western development path" (Liu cited in Ferdinand 2016). In the same way, new foreign policy concepts such as the "new type of international financial institutions" evoke the possibility for China to advocate the necessity of establishing new IFIs such as the AIIB, as well as providing an alternative path to FTAs and economic development through the RCEP. The ideational pillars of Chinese foreign policy presented in this chapter therefore represent the starting point from which to analyse China's position in the global order, through the three major initiatives presented within the book, i.e., the BRI, the AIIB and the RCEP. All three projects need to be examined based on the ideational pillars previously exemplified.

At this stage, China does not seem to be advancing a model of world order that goes against that of major powers in world affairs. From here, some scholars believe China intends to reform and reshape the international order, yet keeping in mind that "the existing international order has actually served the country quite well and its leaders have done much to ensure that they have become a firmly part of it" (Breslin 2013). At the same time, it is in the interests of China to promote ideational resources such as a different type of international relations, a different type of international institutions, and a new model of global governance to integrate further into the existing global order, as well as to provide Chinese leadership, increasing legitimacy at home and abroad.

Bibliography

Ai, Jiawen. 2009. "Two Sides of One Coin: The Party's Attitude Toward Confucianism in Contemporary China." *Journal of Contemporary China* 18 (61): 689–701.

America CGYN. 2017. "Jointly Shoulder Responsibilities of Our Times, Promote Global Growth." Available at https://america.cgtn.com/2017/01/17/full-text-of-xi-jinping-keynote-at-the-world-economic-forum. Accessed 21 October 2017.

Breslin, Shaun. 2013. "China and the Global Order: Signalling Threat or Friendship?" *International Affairs* 89 (3): 615–634.

Breslin, Shaun. 2015. "China's Global Power/China as a Global Power." In *Assessing China's Power*, edited by Jae Ho Chung. Basingstoke: Palgrave Macmillan.

Breslin, Shaun, and Silvia Menegazzi. 2017. "The Chinese Perspective on Global Order." In *Still a Western World? Continuity and Change in Global Order*, edited by Raffaele Marchetti and Sergio Fabbrini. Abingdon: Routledge.

Callahan, Wiliam H. 2015. "History, Tradition and the China Dream: Socialist Modernization in the World of Great Harmony." *Journal of Contemporary China* 24 (96): 983–1001.

Callahan, William H. 2016. "China 2035: From the China Dream to the World Dream." *Global Affairs* 1–12.

Chang, Joseph Y.S. 2016. "Xi Jinping New Model of Major Power Relationships for Sino-American Relations." *Journal of Comparative Asian Development* 15 (2): 226–254.

China.org. 2014, July 7. "Xi's Speech at 'Five Principles of Peaceful Coexistence' Anniversary." Available at http://www.china.org.cn/world/2014-07/07/content_32876905.htm. Accessed 23 May 2017.

China US Focus. 2014, September 24. "Speech at the Opening Ceremony of the International Conference in Commemoration of the 2,565th Anniversary of Confucius' Birth and the Fifth Congress of the Confucian Association." Available at http://library.chinausfocus.com/article-1534.html. Accessed 25 September 2017.

Chinese Cadre Learning Network. 2017, February 21. "Xi Jinping Mentions for the First Time the 'Two Guides' Principle Has Deep Meaning." Available at http://www.ccln.gov.cn/hotnews/230779.shtml (in Chinese). Accessed 5 April 2017.

Dian, Matteo. 2017. *Contested Memories in Chinese and Japanese Foreign Policy.* Oxford: Elsevier.

Ding, Yifan. 2015. "亚投行为什么这么受黄英?" [Why the AIIB Is so Welcome?]. *Guangming Ribao.* Available at http://theory.people.com.cn/n/2015/0319/c40531-26716515.html. Accessed 13 May 2016.

Ferdinand, Peter. 2016. "Westward ho—The China Dream and the 'One Belt One Road': Chinese Foreign Policy under Xi Jinping." *International Affairs* 92 (4): 941–957.

Florini, Ann. 2011. "Rising Asian Powers and Changing Global Governance." *International Studies Review* (13) 1: 24–33.

Goh, Evelyn. 2015. "China's Power in the Regional Context (II): Southeast Asia." In *Assessing China's Power*, edited by Jae Ho Chung. Basingstroke: Palgrave Macmillan.

Katzestein, Peter J. 2012. "China's Rise: Rupture, Return, or Recombination?" In *Sinicization and the Rise of China. Civilizational Processes beyond East and West*, edited by Peter J. Katzenstein. Abingdon: Routledge.

Lampton, David M. 2013. "A New Type of Major-Power Relationship: Seeking a Durable Foundation for US-China Ties." *Asia Policy* 16: 51–68.

Li, He. 2015. *Political Thought and China's Transformation. Ideas Shaping Reform in Post-Mao's China*. New York: Palgrave Macmillan.
Liao, Nien-chung Chang. 2016a. "China's New Foreign Policy Under Xi Jinping." *Asian Security* 12 (2): 82–91.
Liao, Yanfu. 2016b. "中国梦与美国梦的五个差异" [Five Differences between the Chinese Dream and the American Dream]. *Journal of Chongqing University of Post and Telecommunications* 28 (1): 18–24.
Liu, Joanna Liu. 2014. "The Confucian Legacy: A Comparative Studies of the Critical Inheritance of Confucianism in China and North Korea." *Columbia East Asia Review*, 67–94.
Marchetti, Raffaele. 2017. "The Role of Ideas in the Global Order." In *Still a Western World? Continuity and Change in Global Order*, edited by Raffaele Marchetti and Sergio Fabbrini. Abingdon: Routledge.
Ministry of the Foreign Affairs of the People's Republic of China. 2013. "Xi Jinping and US President Obama Hold Joint Press Conference." Available at http://www.fmprc.gov.cn/mfa_eng/topics_665678/xjpttcrmux_665688/t1049545.shtml. Accessed 8 September 2017.
Ministry of the Foreign Affairs of the People's Republic of China. 2016. "构建以合作共赢为核心的新型国际关系" [Constructing New International Relations with Cooperative Win-Win as the Core]. Available at http://www.fmprc.gov.cn/ce/cgct/chn/zgyw/t1247689.htm. Accessed 23 September 2017.
Pan, Yang. 2016. "习近平构建新型国际关系思想初探" [On Xi Jinping's Thought of Constructing New International Relations]. 党史文员 [*Party History*] 12: 66–67.
Qin, Yaqing. 2015. "Culture and Global Thought: Chinese International Theory in the Making." *Revista CIDOB d'Afers Internacionals* 100: 67–89.
Rapkin, David P., and Jonathan R. Strand. 2003. "Is East-Asia under Represented in the International Monetary Found?" *International Relations of the Asia Pacific* 3: 1–28.
Swaine, Micheal. 2014. "Xi Jiping's Address to the Central Conference on Work Relating to the Foreign Affairs: Assessing and Advancing Major-Power Diplomacy with Chinese Characteristics." *China Leadership Monitor* 46: 1–19.
Xiang, Lanxin. 2016. "Xi's Dream and China's Future." *Survival* 58 (3): 53–62.
Xinhua. 2014, June 28. "Chinese President Calls for Greater Democracy in International Relations." Available at http://news.xinhuanet.com/english/china/2014-06/28/c_133445551.htm. Accessed 3 September 2017.
Zhang, Xiaoming. 2015. "需要中国梦与中国梦需要" [The Need of a Chinese Dream and the Needs of the Chinese Dream]. *Gansu Theory Research* 1: 74–77.
Zhang, Xiaoping. 2017. "发展21世纪马克思主义" [Developing Marxism in the XXI Century]. *Chinese Journal of Social Sciences*. Available at http://theory.

gmw.cn/2017-05/26/content_24604712.htm. Accessed 23 September 2017.

Zhao, Suisheng. 2016. "China as a Rising Power versus the US-led World Order." *Rising Powers Quarterly* 1 (1): 13–21.

Zhao, Tingyang. 2006. "Rethinking Empire from a Chinese concept 'All-Under-Heaven' (Tianxia)." *Social Identities* 12 (1): 29–41.

Zhao, Tingyang. 2014. "The 'China Dream' in Question." *Economic and Political Studies* (2) 1: 127–142.

CHAPTER 3

The Asian Infrastructure Investment Bank

Abstract This chapter presents the ideational pillars shaping China's legitimation process concerning major initiatives within regional and global governance. It suggests the idea that the origin, the normative content, and the institutional structures of the initiatives and organizations recently established by China at the regional and global level are vigorously influenced with the way the CCP legitimizes its own ideational narratives in global politics. While arguing so, the chapter analyses two major ideational narratives, post-colonial nationalism and neo-Confucianism. The chapter also examines major political frames through which the Xi Jinping administration is building its legitimacy and strategy while reshaping China's foreign policy: the China Dream, a new type of international relations and a new type of international institutions.

Keywords AIIB · Global economic governance
International financial institutions · Multilateralism

Introduction

The Asian Infrastructure Investment Bank (AIIB) represents a fundamental test for China. Since it is the first time that Beijing has promoted its 'own' international financial institution (IFI), based on its "own" leadership and on its "own" principles, the success of the bank indicates that

M. Dian and S. Menegazzi, *New Regional Initiatives in China's Foreign Policy*, https://doi.org/10.1007/978-3-319-75505-2_3

China is capable of promoting alternative forms of governance to current global and regional institutions, in terms of both membership and rules.

So far, the AIIB has been particularly successful in gathering the support of other partners. Even if the AIIB is considered a regional institution and promotes investments and infrastructures primarily through the Asian region, today half of its members are "non-regionals". Several key European states such as Italy, Germany and France, as well as Asian allies of the US, such as Australia, Philippines and South Korea, are founding members. Adhesion to the Chinese initiative thus appears even more significant, considering the opposition of the US that raised doubts on the transparency and the legal standards of the bidding processes related to the AIIB financing. Similarly, the success of the initiative testifies to an increased and widespread dissatisfaction towards existing global financial institutions. On the one hand, several Asian states lament the incapacity of the Bretton Woods institutions to adapt their internal structure and voting rights to the development of Asian economy. On the other hand, many states favour the creation of forms of governance that are forgiving of hard political and economic conditionality. Another fundamental consequence relates to the normative content of the regional order. The AIIB constitutes a valuable instrument, from a Chinese perspective, to promote its core principles. In this regard, respect for the political sovereignty of, and non-interference in, other states stand as two necessary pre-conditions to the establishment of the AIIB and its membership.

Based on these premises, in this chapter we underpin throughout a more "empirical" example: China's new proposal in light of its vision about the future architecture of global economic governance. In doing so, we will use the AIIB as a case study. While China's growing participation in international financial organizations should not be considered as a breath of fresh air in the domain of global governance, the establishment of the AIIB represents a "critical juncture" to the financial and institutional architecture of the global economic order. Christine Lagarde, IMF Managing Director, declared in March 2015 that the International Monetary Fund—indeed a major institution of the Bretton Woods system—was "delighted" to cooperate with the new China-led organization (Reuters 2015). Two years later, German politicians declared that with the EU seriously supporting the new bank, the AIIB could be transformed into a "true" IFI, which entails however, the guarantee of AIIB not being an institution with "Chinese characteristics" (ECFR 2017).

In this light, the enthusiasm of Western states was unexpected and should not be disregarded.

Chinese leaders were able to exercise a peculiar and unprecedented attraction in the West by an Asian organization, as Japan had done in 1968, with the establishment of the Asian Development Bank. Nevertheless, scepticism also grew in the West, and particularly in the US. From a US perspective, China's initiative to launch its own IFI was the result of China's ascending power at the international level. According to this view, China remains a rising power that needs to be counter-balanced before Western institutions are no longer able to maintain their influence in the world economy. However, the intention here is to avoid the narrative of the so-called "Thucydides's Trap", which portrayed US–China relations as destined for conflict and, most likely war, according to the scholar who theorized it, Graham Allison (2012, 2017). In this light, what follows will show how China's international behaviour and narratives are part of ideational perspectives embedded within daily political discourses that are rooted in China's political tradition and cultural concepts, i.e., neo-Confucianism, or, as emerged most recently, the China Dream. From this point of view, the Chinese narratives about the AIIB present different reasons for why leaders in Beijing decided to launch a new multilateral development bank (MDB), compared to explanations offered by Westerns pundits and media.

Furthermore, this chapter intends to investigate the extent to which China's objective to establish a new IFI was aimed at promoting a leadership role for the country at the regional or global level. A second aim is to understand to what extent Chinese ideas and norms are capable of making a difference with the new initiative. With China's structural transformation from a middle- to a high-income country, the Chinese government is aware of how China requires stronger recognition regarding its role into the world economy. This suggests the need to encompass rules and practices far from China's economic and global governance perspectives. But, on the other hand, it also entails a new attempt to offer valid alternatives to existing norms and institutions. As we shall see, because of China's post-colonial identity, the possibility for Chinese leaders to attract non-Western countries when establishing "a new type of international organizations" has been particularly successful in recent years. This scenario, in parallel with the US will (evident in the Trump administration) to move away from being the major stakeholder *vis-à-vis* economic globalization, has left China additional room for manoeuvre in global governance. In this light, are the origins, the normative content, and the institutional structure of the AIIB, as well as the way the CCP has legitimized political ideas about it, linked to narratives embedded within China's post-colonial nationalism and neo-Confucianism? To what extent does China's ideational narrative remain a valuable resource for our understanding of its foreign policy strategy on unprecedented economic and financial projects, i.e., the AIIB? Are concepts such as the China Dream or a New Type of Major Power Relations of any relevance to our understanding of China's decision to establish the new institution in 2013? These are all questions that will be further discussed and unravelled in the following paragraphs.

AIIB: The Regional Order and Global Governance

July 18, 2017 represents a fundamental moment for the AIIB. It was the day when S&P Global Ratings (S&P) announced the decision to assign their highest possible rating to, and stable outlook for, the bank. According to an S&P report, "over the next three to five years AIIB will establish a track record and significantly enhance its operational setup". More precisely, trust and support from the rating US giant came from the fact that with 80 sovereign members, the AIIB remains today one of the largest multilateral lending institutions globally (S&P 2017).

The AIIB is a multilateral financial institution (MFI) officially inaugurated on 16 January 2016. Although it has more than 57 Western countries among its members, the institution is a China-led organization. In 2013, during a state visit to Indonesia, the Chinese president announced the decision to set up an Asian Infrastructure and Investment Bank "that would give priority to ASEAN countries' needs" (ASEAN-China Centre 2013). While intensions by the Xi Jinping administration to set up a MDB were part of China's regional strategy in both political and economic terms, the new project raised numerous constraints well beyond the Asian region. For instance, according to Shogo Suzuki, framing the issue through the contest of Sino-Japanese rivalry in the region would limit a real understanding of China's deeper intentions to set up the new bank, i.e., its growing dissatisfaction with an American-led financial international order (Suzuki 2015). Since its official launch in October 2014, the new IFI has been perceived in the West as a direct challenge to the existing economic order (Council on Foreign Relations 2015). Anxiety was generated on the one hand by the possibility that the AIIB would undermine existing international aid institutions, overshadowing organizations such as the World Bank or the IMF.

On the other hand, concerns were related to the fact that the AIIB represented living proof of China's intention of playing a larger geopolitical and economic role at the international level. In this sense, Chinese predominance regarding global governance would also, de facto, have directly undermined US hegemony and the existing world order (Lipcy 2015). Even more precisely, today the lively debate on China's engagement with the establishment of a new MDB involves four main considerations: (1) the need to contextualize China's recent action in line with its intention of playing a bigger role within regional and global multilateral organizations; (2) the degree of participation and the efforts Chinese leaders can make in global economic governance; (3) the level of China's institutional statecraft today, and compared with the past; (4) China's "counter-hegemonic" purposes at the institutional/international level (Ikenberry and Lim 2017). According to Ikenberry and Lim, as today's international order is both complex and multilayered, China has no choice but to comply with existing norms, institutions, rules and regimes, although based on its own logic (2017, p. 5). As we shall argue, within such a process it is thus essential to distinguish between the different sources of propagated ideas and political narratives concerning China's role in global economic governance and its institutions. In 2008, Ikenberry was already arguing that the rise of China and the future of the West were unquestionably intertwined. In his view, only two scenarios were contemplated: either China would replace the rules and the institutions of the international system, thus becoming a threat to and a rival of the Western liberal order, or China could largely benefit from it, assuring a smooth power transition and gaining full access and benefits from the international system Western states, i.e., the US, created after World War II (Ikenberry 2008). The narrative however, generally stands in sharp contrast to the way in which Chinese leaders, scholars and intellectuals think about China's growing relevance to the international system. The discourse of power politics and realpolitik dynamics are often discharged by leaders and analysts in the PRC, which instead prefer to contextualize China's behaviour as being the result of different interpretations concerning its culture, civilization and political matters. As such, to understand how they think about China's place in the present global order clearly matters. As Chin explains, the establishment of the new bank is a signal of China's growing frustration in terms of Western leaders' exclusive management within existing international institutions, coupled with a shift in the balance of world economic power at the international level (Chin 2016).

In China, one the most discussed political narratives explaining China's ascent role in international affairs is that framing the debate between Deng Xiaoping's idea of *taoguangyanghui* and China's recent assertiveness since the start of the Millenium. According to such view, it is important to understand why and how China abandoned its low profile and opted instead for ascent participation in world affairs and global governance. In the last two years, discussions about the AIIB have proliferated in academia, yet little evidence has been provided concerning the distinct views on the AIIB held by Chinese scholars. Yet, since 2015, China's discourse on the AIIB has become the end point within all Xi Jinping's foreign policy official speeches. During a state visit he made to the US, he defined the AIIB as "an open and inclusive multilateral development agency" (Wall Street Journal 2015). In 2016, at the AIIB inauguration ceremony, the Chinese President further stressed AIIB's commitment to "open regionalism". While the AIIB is designed to implement investments to support infrastructure development in Asia, the bank is in the same way *open* to collaboration with existing MDBs to reform the global economic governance system (*Xinhua* 2016). The political narrative underpinned by policymakers in Beijing is therefore one which asks whether the new bank is an attempt by China to consolidate its leadership role within the region, or instead, an effort to promote alternative normative rules and practices to a kind of global governance which could be described as having "Chinese characteristics".

As anticipated in Chapter 1, speaking theoretically and more precisely from an English School perspective, the issue also involves understanding where for instance, we are deemed to posit China's role on the pluralist–solidarist spectrum. It is thus necessary to understand which type of international order Chinese leaders envision for the future of global governance. As previously argued, China's identity and foreign policy practices are far from willing to portray a solidarist vision of international order. Rather, in the global governance domain, with China still assigning major priority to norms such as sovereignty and non-interference, a pluralist vision of world order is expected to characterize China's emergence as the economic dominant power, most likely, through institution-building and political narratives.

The Chinese Narrative: AIIB as a New Type of International Financial Institution

The headquarters of the AIIB are in Beijing. It officially inaugurated its activities on January 16, 2016, following the entrance into force of the Articles of Agreement (AoA) on December 25, 2015. The AIIB is often described by different names defining its institutional typology: as a multilateral development bank (MDB), as an international financial institution (IFI) or as a regional investment bank (RIB). These terms have similar but slightly different meanings, and are all applicable to the AIIB; as such, they will are interchangeably within the book. Nevertheless, omitting the questions of definitions, one of the main purposes of the chapter consists of looking at China's ideational narrative to explain AIIB's role and functions regarding global economic governance. Therefore, in what follows, special attention will be given to the views of Chinese academics and experts concerning the AIIB.

In line with the narrative previously exemplified, as the concept of a "new type of major power relations" (新型大国关系 *xinxing daguo guanxi*), the AIIB is often classified as a new type of international financial institution (以个新型的国际金融机构 *yi ge xinxing de guoji jinrong jigou*). Aside from Chinese academics and policymakers, in the West the AIIB is considered to be a different institution because it "represents a new tool of statecraft to build and exert authority, and enhance China's leadership status within the international system" (Ikenberry and Lim 2017). The narrative in the West is focused on the fact that through the AIIB China was able to set up a viable alternative to the liberal economic order and more practically, to the Bretton Woods institutions. In a rather different perspective, the Chinese narrative portrays two major issues regarding the decision to establish a new international financial institution: (1) Beijing's frustration over existing MDBs; and (2) the need to implement infrastructure projects and development in the Asian region, as well as in less developed countries among which emerged the Middle East or Central Asia. As we shall argue, each of the two discourses are relevant because of their correlation to Chinese political narratives, namely post-colonialism, which sees China as the bulwark of developing countries in global governance, and neo-Confucian ideas, which instead assume China's "unique" model of development as a successful developmental approach which could also be extended to neighbouring countries and emerging economies.

This explains why, according to Ding Yifan, China has neither the capacity nor the desire to resemble the American hegemonic role with regard to IFIs. China's intentions are not to replace the Asian Development Bank or the World Bank, but to further supplement the existing international monetary and financial system, in order to cater for the growing economic needs and aid assistance in Asia. In Ding's view, a major point of criticism emerged because many developing countries do not hold the same role within international financial institutions in terms of decision-making procedures (Ding 2015). As such, the Silk Road Fund, the BRICS New Development Bank (NDB) and the AIIB all have the same purpose: to increase the participation of non-Western countries in global economic governance. Similarly, Chen Xinguang, from the Chinese Academy of Social Science, believes that functioning as a new type of international financial institution, the AIIB can provide global public goods with its own rules and through new international mechanisms. Even though China remains the largest shareholder in the bank, it will act responsibly, with the intent to learn from existing financial institutions (Chen 2015). Above all, in less than two years since its establishment, 80 countries have already joined the bank. Nevertheless, the creation of the AIIB—as well as the NDB, the Silk Road Fund and the BRICS Contingent Reserve Agreement (CRA)—is also the result of China's intention to transform international financial instruments based on common but growing divergent interests at the international level, coupled with the intent to preserve normative practices often disregarded today by Western states within supranational institutions, such as full respect of sovereignty, non-interference and self-determination. It is not surprising that among the countries joining the bank in the last year, many are from Africa or the Latin American region, and thus share post-colonial narratives and ideas concerning global affairs with China.

As pointed out by He, the establishment of the AIIB may result in a major shift from a "Western-led governance" (西方治理 *xifang zhili*) to a more inclusive "East-West co-governance" (东西方共同治理 *dongxi fang gongtong zhili*), allowing Beijing further political influence in the region, combined with growing inclusiveness at the international level (He 2015). In this light, although the AIIB is certainly boosting China's economic role in global governance, existing MDBs can also serve different purposes. Above all, according to Zhao and Jin, the relationship between the AIIB and other MDBs is "complementary rather than competitive" (互不而非竞争 *hubu er fei jingzheng*), with no need to increase the politicization of economic issues in terms of global financial institutions (Zhao and Jin 2017). This is because, rather than being operated from a 'great power politics' perspective, the new bank is intended as an essential element for increasing cooperation in the South. The AIIB stands as a powerful supplement to the international development financial system with the purpose of supporting the investment in infrastructure primarily of Asian countries, and with the intent to promote the development of the Asian economies (Liu 2016).

According to Fan Jinyu, the implications of the establishment of the AIIB are not only economic but political. The AIIB represents a supplementary mechanism for infrastructure financing in the Asian region. Even though AIIB's regional members have different beliefs, traditional culture and social systems, the new bank will also guarantee investment projects in areas facing geopolitical risks, and therefore contribute to safeguarding the peace and stability in the region (Fan 2015).

AIIB: Structures and Operating Rules

The structure of the bank is organized alongside three major pillars: the Board of Directors, the Board of Governors and the Senior Management Board (comprising the President and the Vice-president). In 2017, an International Advisory Panel was assembled to oversee the bank's governance structure. Jin Liqun is the first AIIB President—but the presidency of the bank is expected to rotate every five years. US medias in 2017 defined the AIIB's first President as "a banker inspired by Western novelists" (*New York Times* 2017). Born and educated in China, Jin has spent most of his career working for Western institutions such as the World Bank in Washington DC (as an attaché of the Chinese Ministry of Finance) and at the Asian Development Bank (where he served as Vice President from 2003 to 2008).

The highest body in terms of decision-making strategies is the Board of Governors, responsible for establishing the major policies of the bank, and to which each member country is expected to designate two governors (a governor and an alternate governor). Among the numerous functions performed by the board are: the admission and suspension of its members; the increase and decrease of the banks' capital stock; the allocation of net incomes and reserves; and organizing the election of the president, as well as changes in the composition of the Board of Directors and the AoA.

The Board of Directors is responsible for the general operations of the bank, i.e., supervising management and units operations, establishing and monitoring policies, approving the bank's annual plan and its budget. Through the implementation of new investment projects, since February 2017 the board has expanded its personnel with the establishment of three Board Committees: the Audit Committee, the Budget and Human Resources Committee (HRC) and the Policy and Strategies Committee (PSC). The Board of Directors is non-resident. The spirit of innovation is, according to Chin, exemplified by the need to maintain the AIIB as "lean, clean and green". By avoiding certain expenses, i.e., personnel travel, and by accommodating the use of modern communication technology, i.e., through virtual meetings among directors, from the medium to long term, the bank is claiming to be more responsible and becoming an environmentally friendly institution. Within such a framework, the extent to which AIIB non-resident boards improve the bank's ethical behaviour in environmental care is difficult to say.

To discuss AIIB's stance *vis-à-vis* environmental standards is beyond the scope of this book. Yet, the narrative about AIIB's operations over environmental issues remains a fundamental concern in order to understand how China legitimizes specific political strategies and discourses through new institutions operating in the global economy. Among the major criticisms about this is China's unwillingness to respect environmental standards due to Beijing's past reluctance to show full acceptance of the (Western) human rights regime. Today, sceptics still believe that China's NDB will fail to meet the necessary conditions to fully respect environmental protection, resulting in poor human rights' consideration when it comes to the risks associated with the new bank's investments (Summers 2017). Yet, it is precisely such a narrative that leaders and academics in Beijing want to discard when it comes to the AIIB. It is the Western-led discourse concerning political, economic and environmental standards in parallel with China's desire to establish its own international norms that helps us to understand Beijing's decision to set up the new bank. Furthermore, it was precisely this narrative—China's taken-for-granted "lack of commitment" to comply with existing norms in the international order—that led the Xi Jinping administration to launch new initiatives, i.e., the establishment of a new MDB. Similarly, the possibility that China might offer a real alternative to non-Western countries to finding their place in global politics, i.e., within international financial institutions—without threatening the same Western-led world order—implies China's strong commitment to escape from great power politics dynamics, in line with post-colonial nationalist behaviour.

Three thematic priorities are key to determining AIIB projects: sustainable infrastructure, cross-country connectivity and private capital mobilization. The first priority, the intention by the AIIB to achieve "sustainable infrastructure", is related to project financing in developing countries with a specific care of green infrastructure. In the last two years, environmental and social accountability standards have become the main priorities to the bank. However, major concerns have already emerged as to whether the AIIB will be able to achieve positive results. In February 2016, the bank published the document entitled *Environment and Social Framework*. Specifically, the 57 pages trace all the major guidelines about AIIB's rules and practices concerning environmental policies and standards. However, major doubts have already emerged as to how the bank will be able to effectively supervise infrastructure projects while guaranteeing environmental impact assessments' procedures in third countries. Roughly 75% of its investment projects have been co-financed with other MDBs, to some a sign that the AIIB is simply delegating environmental responsibility to its partners (Geary 2017). But, according to the Chinese political narrative carried on through new projects such as the AIIB is, it is precisely such a dichotomy—Western countries as defender of good practices and norms versus non-Western countries as the cause of pollution and bad practices—that China intends to avoid when establishing new initiatives such as the AIIB.

AIIB's second priority concerns the prioritization of cross-country infrastructure, i.e., ports, roads and rails across Central Asia, South East Asia, and the Middle East up to the European region. To many, this necessity has grown in parallel with China's deep motivation to create the AIIB. According to American pundits, China's economic foreign policy re-orientation in the Xi Jinping era is structured alongside the main goal of strengthening economic, security and political ties, which explains the creation of the AIIB with a focus on China's neighbours (Weiss 2017). It should be noted that most of the countries taking stock of AIIB project financing are also BRI countries.

Among them, most likely numerous Chinese firms, and particularly State Owned Enterprises (SOEs), are expected to play a key role. In line with China's normative practices regarding market rules, and often against neoliberal models, this is aimed at creating a favourable contest for its own SOEs.

The third priority takes care of innovative solutions to catalyse private capital, specifically, in partnership with other MDBs, governments and other private financiers. Similarly, the intention to attract private capital in the AIIB as a source of financing AIIB's infrastructure projects can be partially explained by the BRI. Because this initiative is aimed at boosting economic connectivity of the Chinese enterprises abroad—implementing China's "going out" strategy and thus, the internationalization of Chinese companies on foreign territories—to attract private capital for infrastructure projects will also benefit the status of the Chinese economy, therefore becoming a key priority for the Xi Jinping administration.

Projects

Since its establishment, the AIIB has devoted considerable effort to providing transparency in terms of how projects are financed. AIIB's projects financing process is guided by six steps: (1) strategic programming; (2) project identification; (3) project preparation; (4) board approval; (5) project implementation; and (6) project completion and evaluation. To date (October 2017), a total of 18 projects has already been approved, although the number is expected to grow in the years ahead. The majority of these are in the Southeast Asia region and the Middle East in the field of energy and transport (see Table 3.1). AIIB's strategy for project financing involves three main beneficiaries. The first concerns *sovereignty-backed financing*, whereby the agent receiving AIIB's partial loans or a fully financed project is a sovereign state, i.e., a member of the bank. The second is the form of *non-sovereign-backed-financing*, whereby beneficiaries can be private enterprises as well as sub-sovereign entities, i.e., defined by the AoA as a political or administrative sub-division of a Member state or a public sector entity. The third strategy concerns *equity investment*, which are intended as investments for companies operating in both the private and the public sectors. Project financing has been a major issue since the AIIB was established back in 2015.

Table 3.1 AIIB approved projects (*source* AIIB.org)

Project name	*Country*	*Sector*	*Co-financed by*	*AIIB financing (million)*
Metro Manila Flood Management Project	Philippines	Water	World Bank	US$ 207.63
IFC Emerging Asia Fund	Asia	Multi-sector	Other investors	US$ 150
Transmission System Strengthening Project	India	Energy	Asian Development Bank	US$ 100
Round II Solar PV Feed-in Tariffs Program	Egypt	Energy	Co-financiers in a syndicate	US$ 210
Gujarat Rural Roads Project	India	Transport	none	US$ 329
Nurek Hydropower Rehabilitation Project	Tajikistan	Energy	World Bank, Eurasian Development Bank	US$ 60
India Infrastructure Fund	India	Multi-sector	TBA (other investors)	Up to US$ 150
Batumi Bypass Road Project	Georgia	Transport	Asian Development Bank	US$ 114
Andhra Pradesh 24x7—Power for All	India	Energy	World Bank	US$ 160
Natural Gas Infrastructure and Efficiency Improvement Project	Bangladesh	Energy	Asian Development Bank	US$ 60
Dam Operational Improvement and Safety Project Phase II	Indonesia	Multi-sector	World Bank	US$ 125
Regional Infrastructure Development Fund Project	Indonesia	Urban	World Bank	US$ 100
Trans Anatolian Natural Gas Pipeline Project	Azerbaijan	Energy	World Bank, Asian Development Bank, EBRD, EIB	US$ 600

(continued)

Table 3.1 (continued)

Project name	*Country*	*Sector*	*Co-financed by*	*AIIB financing (million)*
Duqm Port Commercial Terminal and Operational Zone Development Project	Oman	Transport	SEZAD	US$ 265
Railway System Preparation Project	Oman	Transport	OGLG	US$ 36
Myingyan Power Plant Project	Myanmar	Energy	IFC, Asian Development Bank	US$ 20
Tarbela 5 Hydropower Extension Project	Pakistan	Energy	World Bank	US$ 300
National Slum Upgrading Project	Indonesia	Urban	World Bank	US$ 216.50
National Motorway M-4 Project	Pakistan	Transport	ADB, Department for International Development (UK)	US$ 100
Distribution System Upgrade and Expansion Project	Bangladesh	Energy	None	US$ 165
Dushanbe-Uzbekistan Border Road Improvement Project	Tajikistan	Transport	EBRD	US$ 27.5

AIIB Amid (Chinese) Sovereignty and State Capitalism

As with the other two projects analysed within the book—the BRI and the RCEP—the AIIB manifests China's intention to offer a valid alternative in terms of institution-building through the regional economic and financial order. As such, the result is that a process of contestation is taking place, one in which China's economic model aims to co-exist with Western rules and practices, but with no disruption of taken-for-granted procedures previously established by existing MDBs. More specifically, the process entails the necessity to generate an international environment in which China's economic and political interests are guaranteed by supranational multilateral institutions that extend well beyond Chinese boarders. Such a perspective also results from a direct challenge to key primary institutions, i.e., great power management and the market. From a theoretical perspective, our benchmark in this case is, again, the solidarist–pluralist spectrum within which we intend to place China's behaviour around the AIIB initiative. The pluralist vision maintained by China is fed by the assumption that there should be no limits or any conditions placed on the state's internal and political sovereignty. On the issue of sovereignty, we find evidence in the Article 31, paragraph 2 of the AIIB AoA claiming that:

> The Bank, its President, officers and staff should not interfere in the political affairs of any member, nor shall they be influenced in their decisions by the political character of the member concerned. Only economic considerations shall be relevant to their decisions. Such considerations shall be weighed impartially in order to achieve and carry out the purpose and functions of the bank. (AIIB Articles of Agreement)

The idea that AIIB's member countries should comply to fully respect each other's sovereignty gives the bank a different political outlook as compared with previous established MDBs. Yet, China's behaviour over the world's multilateral economic architecture should not be viewed merely as a disruptive factor in the global governance scenario. Rather, it is part of a more global trend resulting from a revolution that started in the last decade and which saw the involvement of non-Western countries within the multilateral development regime on a steady rise. According to Ngaire Woods, for instance, China is among the major donors providing developmental assistance to rogue states with no conditionality.

As with the situation in the global economic governance domain, emerging donors, i.e., China, strongly defend sovereignty and non-interference in the politics of recipients of their aids. A further similarity concerns the consequences of such a *silent* revolution envisioned by Woods: emerging donors are not attempting to overturn the rules of the developmental assistance regime; rather, they are attempting to offer an alternative to aid-receiving countries, at the same time generating competitive pressure within the existing regimes (Woods 2008). A great deal of evidence of this type allows us to argue not only that China's post-colonial identity is on the rise, but that the consequences at the global level are unprecedented: never before has a non-Western country been able to exercise such a level of relative attractiveness to global economic governance within, but especially outside, Western contexts. The result is that, at a time when the Bretton Woods architecture is continuously under scrutiny, neoliberal ideas and concepts about economic rules and norms have lost some of their attraction for the Chinese narrative, which, de facto, has increasingly become more attractive to new players outside (but not confined to) Western contexts.

In a similar way, through AIIB's financing of projects, we might also expect China's state capitalism to be on the rise. As previously exemplified, we conceive state capitalism as Beijing's intentions to promote not only market regulation based on Chinese needs, but more specifically, the systematic promotion of China's SOEs abroad, with China's political and economic interests improving too. To date, the majority of AIIB's financed projects have grown in parallel with other projects financed or being developed along the New Silk Road. The idea beyond the strategy is one in which, through the AIIB Chinese companies, will have at their disposal an international platform to further globalize. One thinks, for instance, of the port of Gwadar, based in the tiny but highly strategic Balochistan province of Pakistan. Just as it happened with the Chinese presence in the port of Piraeus (Greece), in 2013 Chinese SOEs began to play a decisive role in the soil surrounding the port area, i.e., thanks to massive investments and an immense jobs business plan promised to the Pakistani government by the Xi Jinping administration. Moreover, it is through the China–Pakistan Economic Corridor (CPEC) that state capitalism can be seen to be expanding. In April 2017, the Pakistani government agreed to hand over all the operations of Pakistan's strategic Gwadar port to a Chinese SOE, the China Overseas Port Holding Company (COPHC). This company has been charged with conducting all infrastructure work at the Arab port for a period of 40 years (*The Economic Times* 2017). COPHC holds a 91% share of revenue collection from gross revenue of terminal and marine operations, and an 85% share of gross revenues from free zone cooperation. According to the Minister for Ports and Shipments, the Pakistani government does not have any share in revenue collection. Estimates believe such form of state capitalism *a la Chinoise* is expected to highly boost employment figures in the area, i.e., the creation of more than 700,000 jobs in Pakistan (*The Nation* 2017). AIIB's AoA make no mention of the actors/beneficiaries employed in infrastructure building activities. However, the case of the Gwadar port in the Balochistan province leads us to believe that Chinese SOE enterprises will play a bigger role than any other foreign firms (if any) involved in infrastructure-building.

Conclusion

Since its official launch in 2016, the AIIB has represented a valid alternative to existing MDBs. In the beginning, fears by Western countries were exacerbated by the idea that the AIIB would pose a significant challenge to Western institutions such as the World Bank or the ADB. However, in a period of less than two years, fear has given way to cooperation and even to an apparent win-win scenario. Practically speaking, most projects are not only financed by the AIIB but co-financed together with other IFIs, such as WB, ADB, and EBRD. While it is true that China ultimately maintains the power of veto over major decisions, Beijing politics in the bank do not sound too "nationalistic" regarding how decisions are made about when projects are financed or by whom. The attractiveness of the AIIB among Western states and non-regional members is also on the rise. In March 2017, the bank approved 13 new members, among which those from outside the Asian region (so-called non-regional prospective members), accounted for 8 out of 13. In May 2017, another seven members joined the bank, among which non-regional members once again represented the majority, i.e., Greece, Romania, Chile and Bolivia. The ongoing membership expansion of the bank is a clear sign of the political narrative underpinned by the AIIB, which appears to support the Chinese political "philosophy" to aspire for highly inclusive global economic governance.

Likewise, it is also in line with the China post-colonial identity and neo-Confucian narratives. While the majority (if not all) of the countries taking advantage of AIIB's infrastructure projects are BRI countries, the growing inclusiveness of the AIIB, in parallel with China's benevolent leadership role within the bank, depicts an image of the Beijing government in stark contrast with the criticisms levelled against major international institutions concerning their complete lack of attention to developing countries and emerging economies. This, as previously mentioned, is also part of a global trend, which is not confined to the domain of IFIs. Therefore, China's post-colonial identity has been able to attract numerous countries within the bank, despite scepticism about the unequal power held by China, compared with other members. Similarly, the political narrative presented by the AIIB, one that saw a new MDB established to increase the peaceful development of the East Asian region, is precisely part of that neo-Confucian perspective that has been promoted by the Xi Jinping administration since he came to power in late 2012. Despite the fact that the global governance scenario in which the AIIB was established has always been ripe for rivalry, China's massive increase in development finance provides a valid alternative to Western-dominated institutions. It is perhaps too early to tell whether the new bank will able to keep expectations high, so as to fully comply with international norms and standards, while continuing infrastructure projects in developing countries. However, Western-led institutions will most likely see their role in global economic governance challenged, at least partially, by China's ability to contest the regional and global order without being trapped into great power politics dynamics.

Bibliography

AIIB. 2015. "Asian Infrastructure and Investment Bank Articles of Agreement." https://www.aiib.org/en/about-aiib/basic-documents/_download/articles-of-agreement/basic_document_english-bank_articles_of_agreement.pdf. Accessed 25 September 2017.

Allison, Graham T. 2012. "Thucydides's has been sprung in the Pacific." Available at https://www.ft.com/content/5d695b5a-ead3-11e1-984b-00144feab49a.

Allison, Graham T. 2017. *Destined for War: Can America and China Escape Thucydides's Trap?* Boston, MA: Houghton Mifflin Harcourt.

ASEAN-China Centre. 2013. "Speech by Chinese President Xi Jinping to Indonesia Parliament." Available at http://www.asean-china-center.org/english/2013-10/03/c_133062675.htm.

Chen, Xinguang. 2015. "亚投行充分展示中国影响力" [AIIB Fully Demonstrates China's Influence]. Available at http://column.chinadaily.com.cn/article.php?pid=5393.

Chin, Gregory T. 2016. "Asian Infrastructure Investment Bank: Governance Innovation and Prospects." *Global Governance* 22 (1): 11–26.

Council on Foreign Relations. 2015, March 17. "A Bank Too Far?" Available at https://www.cfr.org/interview/bank-too-far. Accessed 23 August 2017.

Ding, Yifan. 2015. "亚投行为什么这么受黄英?" [Why the AIIB Is so Welcome?] *Guangming Ribao*. Available at http://theory.people.com.cn/n/2015/0319/c40531-26716515.html. Accessed 13 May 2016.

Fan, Jinyu. 2015. "亚投行风险控制对此建议" [Suggestions about Risks Control Measures of the AIIB]. "投资与合作" [*Investment and Cooperation*] 8 (254): 59–60.

Full Transcript: Interview with Chinese President Xi Jinping. 2015. Available at https://www.wsj.com/articles/fulltranscript-interview-with-chinese-president-xi-jinping-1442894700.

Geary, Kate. 2017. "China's AIIB Is about 2 Face Two Major Tests." *The Diplomat*. http://thediplomat.com/2017/06/chinas-aiib-is-about-to-face-2-major-tests/.

He, Y. 2015. '从"西方治理"到"东西方共治"' (From 'Western governance' to 'East-West co-governance'), Caixin.com, April 6, 2015. Available at http://weekly.caixin.com/2015-04-03/100797317.html.

Ikenberry, G. John. 2008. "The Rise of China and the Future of the West: Can the Liberal System Survive?" *Foreign Affairs* 87 (1): 23–37.

Ikenberry, G. John, and Darren J. Lim. 2017. "China's Emerging Institutional Statecraft. The Asian Infrastructure Investment Bank and the Prospects for Counter-Hegemony." Brookings.

Lipcy, Phillip Y. 2015, May 7. "Who's Afraid of the AIIB: Why the United States Should Support China's Asian Infrastructure Investment Bank." *Foreign Affairs*. Available at https://www.foreignaffairs.com/articles/china/2015-05-07/whos-afraid-aiib. Accessed 3 September 2016.

Liu, Xiangfen. 2016. "亚投行在国际发展融资体系中将成为重要支柱" [The AIIB Will Become an Important Pillar in the International Development Financing System]. "全球化" [*Globalization*] 6: 32–43.

Patton, Dominique. 2015. "IMF Happy to Cooperate with China on AIIB: Lagarde." Available at http://www.reuters.com/article/us-china-imf/imf-happy-to-cooperate-with-china-on-aiib-lagarde-idUSKBN0MI06J20150322. Accessed 29 October 2016.

S&P Global Rating. 2017. Rating Direct. Asian Infrastructure Investment Bank Assigned 'AAA/A-1' Rating; Outlook Stable. Available at https://www.aiib.org/en/news-events/news/2017/_download/20170718_001.pdf.

Stanzel, Angela. 2017. "A German View of the Asian Infrastructure Investment Bank." Available at http://www.ecfr.eu/article/commentary_a_german_view_of_the_aiib_7275. Accessed 25 May 2017.

Summers, Elizabeth. 2017, June 8. "AIIB Must Do More to Meet Its Environmental and Social Commitments." Business and Human Rights Resource Centre. Available at https://business-humanrights.org/en/civil-society-analysis-finds-aiib-access-to-information-policy-needs-improvement-c158594. Accessed 23 September 2017.

Suzuki, Shogo. 2015. "Will the AIIB Trigger Off a New Round of Rivalry in Economic Diplomacy between China and Japan?" CSRG Working Paper 279/15. Available at https://www2.warwick.ac.uk/fac/soc/pais/research/researchcentres/csgr/papers/279-15.pdf. Accessed 26 September 2016.

The Economic Times. 2017, April 20. "Pakistan's Gwadar Port Leased to Chinese Companies for 40 Years." Available at http://economictimes.indiatimes.com/news/international/world-news/pakistans-gwadar-port-leased-to-chinese-company-for-40-years/articleshow/58284735.cms. Accessed 28 September 2017.

The Nation. 2017, April 20. "Gwadar Port Leased to Chinese Company for 40 Years, Senate Told." Available at http://nation.com.pk/business/20-Apr-2017/gwadar-port-leased-to-chinese-company-for-40-years-senate-told. Accessed 25 May 2017.

The New York Times. 2017, January 13. "A Banker Inspired by Western Novelists Seeks to Build Asia." *The New York Times*. Available at https://www.nytimes.com/2017/01/13/world/asia/china-aiib-jin-liqun.html. Accessed 23 September 2017.

Weiss, Martin A. 2017. "Asian Infrastructure Investment Bank." Congressional Research Service, pp. 1–22.

Woods, Ngaire. 2008. "Whose Aid? Whose Influence? China, Emerging Donors and the Silent Revolution in Development Assistance." *International Affairs* 84 (6): 1205–1221.

Xinhua. 2016, January 16. "Full Text of Chinese President Xi Jinping's Address at AIIB Inauguration Ceremony." *Xinhua*. Available at http://news.xinhuanet.com/english/china/2016-01/16/c_135015661.htm. Accessed 23 May 2017.

Zhao, Jun, and Jing Jin. 2017. "亚投行与现衔多边开发银行的关系定位屈清和协调" [The Position, Clarification and Coordination of the Relationship between the AIIB and Existing Multilateral Development Banks]. "太平洋学报" [*Pacific Journal*] 25 (5): 23–33.

CHAPTER 4

Belt and Road, State Capitalism and China's Economic Interests

Abstract This chapter describes how the BRI contributes to contest several elements of the current regional order in Asia. BRI is the most evident attempt to design a leadership role for China. Moreover, it contributes to the Westword re-orientation of the Chinese foreign policy from the East Asian region to the Eurasian continent. BRI also represents a fundamental step in the process of contestation of the market as regional primary institution, through the advancement of state capitalist practices. Finally, the chapter discusses the relationship between the BRI and the Chinese understanding of the international order. BRI contributes to edify a regional order closer to the Chinese preferences, but it also creates the premises for a Chinese foreign policy in contradiction with the practice of non-interference and respect of sovereignty.

Keywords Belt and Road Initiative · Connectivity · Infrastructures
Eurasia · State capitalism · Non interference · Neo-Confucianism

The Chinese Narrative and the BRI

The Belt and Road Initiative—BRI (一带一路 *yidaiyilu*) is the epitome of the high esteem in which the Chinese leadership has held political ideas and concepts in the twenty-first century. According to Yu Jie, the BRI "narrative" follows previous memorable slogans such as "Peaceful Rise", "Harmonious World", or "New Great Power Relations" (Yu 2017). Furthermore,

M. Dian and S. Menegazzi, *New Regional Initiatives in China's Foreign Policy*, https://doi.org/10.1007/978-3-319-75505-2_4

a key issue raised by the Chinese scholar is linked to the lack of a deeper investigation by pundits and China experts when analysing specifically how the B&R has been "ideated", by whom is administered, and how further advancements, in terms of strategies and projects, are supposed to be implemented in the future. More specifically, inside the Chinese political-administrative apparatus, a lack of policy coordination and bureaucratic management is one of the major problems related to the B&R, mainly because the initiative is jointly administered by the National Development and Reform Commission (NDRC), the Ministry of Commerce (MOFCOM), the Ministry of Foreign Affairs (MFA) and an ad hoc "Small Leading Group", which establish how major decisions are taken regarding the BRI (Yu 2017).

It is vital in studies of Chinese foreign policy to understand how and by whom key policy issues are organized, as well as how foreign policy decisions are made in China. This is because, as explained by Jakobson and Manuel, with the growing number of actors involved in China's international activities, authority has become "fractured" in foreign policy decision-making (2016). Yet, since 2012, Xi Jinping has resumed charge of all foreign policy activities and strategies, one of whose main aims is to become the principal coordinator of all interest groups, and the B&R is no exception. To this extent, the so-called "Silk Road Economic Diplomacy" is precisely "the signature foreign policy proposal of Xi, and in some sense, can be seen as the economic pillar of Xi's strategy to rejuvenating China on the world stage" (Zhang 2016).

Despite Chinese economic and geopolitical interests to promote the BRI, the ideational narrative behind this requires further attention, as it represents a clear message delivered by China's core leader about the future strategy for its country abroad—as well as within its own borders:

> We should pursue the Belt and Road Initiative as a priority, give equal emphasis to 'bringing in' and 'going global', follow the principle of achieving shared growth through discussion and collaboration, and increase openness and cooperation in building innovation capacity. With these efforts, we hope to make new ground in opening China further through links running eastward and westward, across land and over sea. (CSIS Reconnecting Asia 2017)

The BRI did not come out of the blue from Xi Jinping's administration. Rather, it is the result of a new kind of "infrastructure diplomacy", with roots in other projects predating 2013. The idea of having the Eurasian continent "all connected" through infrastructure development has been promoted for decades by Western multilateral institutions such as the Asian Development Bank or the European Union (Rolland 2017). In this sense, China's attempt to connect the Asian continent to Europe through infrastructure networks is nothing new. This is precisely why we need to look at the Chinese narrative with the aim of underscoring new insights about the real motivation guiding Xi Jinping's ideas in terms of China's foreign policy.

At this stage, it is worth highlighting the two main intellectual narratives presented in the course of this volume as a point of reference to understanding China's present role in regional and global economic governance: post-colonial nationalism and neo-Confucianism. As for the latter, China is ready to promote economic integration and globalization at a time in which Western states struggle to maintain their status as the only providers of global public goods. In this light, framed as "a new frontier for win-win cooperation", the BRI is portrayed as a significant platform that can strengthen, with positive results, major risks undermining the world economy. Ruan Zongze described the BRI as "the Chinese prescription" for resolving the fragility and uncertainty of the world economy as well as the lack of uncoordinated global economic policies at the international level" (Ruan 2017). At the same time, Ruan underlines the B&R's scope to be "the key driver for emerging economies and developing countries to facilitate global infrastructure construction, promote world economic growth and improve the reform of the international global economic governance" (Ruan 2017). In sum, Ruan's analysis is in line with the double narrative previously exemplified, one in which China is simultaneously portrayed as the new catalyst of the world's economy, but without disrupting the existing financial and economic architecture, and especially with the inclusion of those countries previously forgotten or excluded by the great Western powers. The BRI offers an essential argument for Beijing leaders to portray an image of China, at the international level, as a major actor in the global economic governance, but with a new identity when compared with its predecessors.

BRI occupies therefore an essential position in the Chinese narrative. The very evocation of the Silk Road spirit and the image on the Silk Roads connecting China with the rest of Asia, the Middle East and Europe evokes a form of Chinese exceptionalism. Coherently with the

Neo-Confucian ideas, the rise of China is not destined to trigger great power competition and security dilemmas. On the contrary the renewed Chinese centrality, alimented by the BRI, is destined to be a factor of stability, growth and harmony for the region and the world:

> China adheres to the fundamental national policy of opening up and pursues development with its doors open wide. China will actively promote international cooperation through the 'Belt and Road Initiative'. In doing so, we hope to achieve policy, infrastructure, trade, financial, and people-to-people connectivity and thus build a new platform for international cooperation to create new drivers of shared development. (CSIS Reconnecting Asia 2017)

In this sense through BRI, China is returning to its legitimate position, at the centre of the region. As stated by Major General Qiao Liang "the BRI has a *Tianxia* feeling" (Rolland 2017, p. 135). In this sense BRI is presented more as a rightful return to a natural position of leadership, rather than the manifestation of a new rising power. China's approach, inspired to non-interference and win-win solutions in this sense is presented as inspired both to the Confucian ideas of "humane authority and wisdom" and the special understanding of the conditions of developing Asian countries, due to the Chinese own experience of development and anti-imperialist struggle. The idea of a regional order based on neo-Confucian concepts entails both the capacity to overcome difference and tolerate diversity and the recognition of a Chinese centrality as "order maker," at least in Asia and beyond (Kallio 2016).

Ultimately BRI is also, as William Callahan has stated, a strategy aimed at "build[ing] a tight network of economic, cultural, political and security relations," with the objective of "socializ[ing] Asia and Europe into its own preferred view of global order." (Callahan 2016).

Belt and Road, State Capitalism and China's Economic Interests

The relevance of the Belt and Road Initiative (BRI) goes beyond its capacity to legitimize China's rise and possible leadership role in Asia, placing it within a narrative rooted in neo-Confucian and post-colonial elements. The BRI has also been driven by fundamental economic and political rationales.

The BRI initiative was conceived to improve and strengthen the activities of Chinese SOEs at the global level, as confirmed by Jack Ma, the Chinese business magnate and founder and CEO of the Alibaba Group. In line with the Chinese narrative, Ma believes the BRI will be able to reinforce the economy of small and developing countries. At the same time, he stresses that it will provide Chinese enterprises with more opportunities outside China, i.e., in Malaysia, and that the Alibaba Group is particularly interested in playing a role within it. This is a clear sign that the BRI is expected to further expand from the level of connectivity, through infrastructure development, up to the information technology level (Xinhuanet 2017a).

From the point of view of relations between state and market, BRI has several broad functions: the resistance to Western style free-market capitalism; the survival and consolidation of state capitalism as the economic foundation of the Chinese path to development; and internationalization, through the expansion of the Chinese economic clout. From our theoretical point of view, this can be interpreted as a process of contestation of the "market" as a primary institution of regional order. While China does not aim to export this model of state capitalism, the institutionalization of forms of economic integration firmly rooted in state-led, infrastructure-driven development has the consequence of spreading the practices associated with it. From this perspective, BRI represents the continuation and an expansion of several policies promoted by the Third and Fourth Generations of Leaders: the process of restructuration and consolidation of the state sector initiated by Zhu Rongji[1] and the go-out policy, started in 1999.

The first rationale regards China's economic model of development and its relationship with the Chinese political system. Since the Deng Era, the People's Republic has embraced an export-oriented model characterized by high levels of investments and low levels of private consumption. Since the 1990s, the market has assumed a progressively more central role in the Chinese economy, with the privatization of a great part of the state-owned economy. Chinese policymakers followed the famous catch phrase "grasp the large, release the small" (*zhuda, fangxiao*) which, at the time, was perceived as a commitment to a transition from socialism to fully-fledged free-market capitalism. However, the

[1] Zhu Rongji was premier of the PRC between 1998 and 2003.

intention of the Chinese government was to build a dual system in which the market regulated non-strategic industries, while the state retained control of sectors that were considered strategic for the Chinese national interest. In other terms, the process led to the creation of a state capitalist system (Heilmann and Shih 2013).

This process started in 1994, when the government promoted the new Company Law and reforms aimed at the "corporatization" of state industries. During this period, compulsory planning was eliminated and all SOEs were forced to restructure into corporations, adapting to the rule of market economy. In the decade following 1993, the size of the state sector shrunk dramatically in absolute terms, and even more when compared with the total size of the economy (Hsieh and Zheng 2015).

The "releasing the small" phase came with very significant social costs. According to data released by the Chinese Ministry of Labour and Social Security, 37 million workers were laid off from SOEs between 1994 and 2004, with the total number of state employees falling from a peak of 113 million in 1995 to 88 million in 1998 and 64 million in 2004 (Cai et al. 2008). The process of restructuration and privatization considerably slowed down in 2003, with the creation of the State Asset Supervision and Administration Commission (SASAC), an organ of the State Council charged with the task of managing the largest national (non-financial) state-owned enterprises (Naughton 2015).

The process of privatization and corporatization led to the emergence of a tiered system. The top tier is characterized by the "commanding heights" of the economy and consists of sectors that are considered strategic for the Chinese economy and for national security. These include, energy, oil, telecommunications, transportation, construction, aviation and, significantly, banking. The top tier is constituted largely by large state-owned enterprises that generally act like monopolies or oligopolies, and enjoy special legislative and financial treatment.

The middle tier is constituted by a mix of private and public ownership. Typically, this segment comprises pharmaceuticals, industrial machineries, chemical, automobiles, and technological equipment. Firms in this segment are not considered crucial to national security. They are normally integrated into international supply chains of production and joint ventures. Despite this, it is often hard to determine whether middle-tier companies, for instance Huawei, are entirely independent from the government. Finally, the third tier is constituted by the small and large private enterprises in light industries and agriculture.

These sectors are generally characterized by private property and market dynamics (Pearson 2015).

This economic model consolidated the Party's grip on the economy and allowed the going out policy. The main purposes of that policy were access to raw materials, acquisition of foreign technology and know-how, and improvement of the level of competitiveness of Chinese firms (US-China Economic and Security Review Commission 2011). The going out policy led to an exponential rise in outbound foreign direct investment from less than a billion USD in 2000 to 56 billion in 2006, finally reaching 183 billion in 2016 (UNCTAD 2017).

Chinese outbound direct investments have been historically very diversified, with a substantial portion directed to developed countries, with the aim of acquiring financial assets and foreign technology, and the rest directed to the developing world, with the aim of securing raw materials and acquiring political influence. SOEs have been at the centre of the going out strategy for several reasons. SOEs could face the high costs and the potential risks associated with a policy of long-term investments abroad, with fewer concerns about short-term profitability. Secondly, the going out policy itself was considered essential in the process of creating a base of strategic national champions (Shambaugh 2013).

Despite the process of reform and consolidation of the state sector, the Chinese leadership continued to fear for the viability of the dual model based on a strong role of the SOEs. Many analysts, especially in the West, underlined the need to complete the process of liberalization of the Chinese economy, advancing the painful, but necessary, transition from an export-oriented model, based on high levels of investment, to a consumption- and service-oriented model. However, the Chinese leadership was aware of the economic and social costs of this type of transition. Moreover, a further downsizing of the state sector could deprive the Party of an instrument of control over the national economy and Chinese society.

These fears were particularly present after the 2008 global financial crisis, which led to a decline of the global demand for Chinese goods (Lardy 2012). Beijing responded to the crisis with a massive economic stimulus that was channelled mainly through state-owned banks and SOEs. Moreover, in 2009, the government identified 30 "national champions" that received 10 billion USD under the plan for revitalization of the state industry (Wong 2011).

In the aftermath of the crisis, analysts identified a new trend, the "the expansion of the state, and the retreat of private (*guojin mintui* 国进民退) (Breslin 2010; Eaton 2013). Rather than choosing the path of economic restructuring, Beijing preferred to use the economic stimulus to maintain a high level of growth, while reinforcing the state sector. In practical terms, this meant a renewed emphasis on infrastructure investments that became, even more than in the past, a key driver for economic growth. The emphasis on infrastructure had another fundamental advantage: it directly benefited top-level SOEs that concentrated their activities in sectors such as transport, steel, concrete, telecommunications, shipping, and energy (Naughton 2016b). This renewed gamble on the state capitalist model was confirmed by the 18th Party Congress in November 2013. The Congress led to several reforms aimed at allowing the market to "play a decisive role in allocating national resources", as well as to "encourage, support and guide the non-publicly owned economy". Nevertheless, the same congress also restated the "leading role of the state owned economy" (Rolland 2017).

It is no coincidence that the BRI was unveiled immediately after the 18th Party Congress, when the Party decided to further consolidate the state sector, stressing its fundamental strategic role in pursuing China's economic progress and national interests. Consequently, the BRI aimed to address several problems caused by the fact that SOEs had responded to both political and economic incentives. First, the BRI addressed the problem of overcapacity of Chinese state industries, especially in sectors such as steel, cement, coal and aluminium, rubber and solar plants.

Market distortions generated by preferential legislative treatment and facilitated access to credit, together with political incentives, led to a situation in which main SOEs tried to increase their market share and total industrial output, at the expense of profitability. This led to a "commodity glut", a constant expansion of the supply of commodities which, in turn, led to a sharp decline in prices, forcing many SOEs to sell their products below the cost price. This created problems of debt and sustainability both for SOEs and the banks supporting them (Leutert 2016; Shen and Chen 2017).

As the Chinese territory started to become saturated with new large infrastructural projects, the Party and the SASAC were faced with a choice: to either downsize, as a means of reducing excess productive capacity, or to find new projects for the Chinese SOEs. In this respect, the opportunities offered by the BRI were timely. The possibility of starting a vast array of new projects would contribute both to addressing the issue of overcapacity and bringing about a higher demand for commodities, thus driving prices up, avoiding a painful process of restructuration and marketization of several large SOEs, as well as the political consequences of political infighting and popular resentment. The necessity to consider reducing the size and the role of central SOEs was probably associated with the memories of the reforms promoted by Zhu Rongji's policy of "grasping the large and letting the small go", in the 1990s. While these reforms are now generally considered as both successful and instrumental in the high level of growth China experienced in the following years, they also incurred related costs, since the marketization and the privatization of non-strategic sectors led to the layoff of millions of workers.

Ultimately, the BRI is considered necessary to help the process of consolidation of core SOEs, which, according to Xi's words must have "a dominant role in important sectors and crucial areas that affect national security and the commanding heights of the economy" (Naughton 2016a, p. 18). The launch of the BRI was accompanied by a process of merger and acquisition that favoured the creation of even bigger industrial conglomerates. Examples are the mergers between the South and North China Railway companies and the China Railway Rolling Stock Corporation, and the China Ocean Shipping Group Company (China Shipping Group), the logistic group Sino-Trans and China Merchant Group into a unique conglomerate called China COSCO Shipping Corporation (Wildau 2017; Godement and Leutert 2016). Moreover, the Chinese government and SASAC ceased the practice of making central and provincial SOEs compete with each other to obtain infrastructure contracts. Since BRI bidding processes are, at least formally, open to non-Chinese firms, SASAC decided to avoid competition between national SOEs, with the objective of maximizing Chinese influence (Leutert 2016).

The consolidation of SOEs not only serves domestic purposes, it also helps to build long-term influence in the countries that receive Chinese investments within the BRI framework. It is no coincidence that Xi and the rest of the leaders, during their "BRI diplomatic tours" between 2014 and 2016, particularly emphasized the role of high-speed trains and shipping. On the one hand, they represented the symbols of the BRI as an unprecedented project based on connectivity and economic integration. On the other hand, they embodied the type of investment China prefers. Building heavy infrastructures in the sea and land transport sectors, is a very effective way to contribute to the regeneration of central SOEs.[2]

The BRI may also have a positive impact on the Chinese banking and financial system, especially in the role of main public banks. The outflow of investments related to the BRI is destined to further enhance the relationship between the five main state-owned banks and central SOEs, as well as increasing their control by the government and the Party (Elliott and Yan 2013; Peck and Zhang 2013). Overall, a significant portion of infrastructural projects promoted under the banner of the BRI will be managed by central SOEs, supported by main public banks and preferential legislative treatment (Zhong 2017).

This is likely to have two main impacts. First, politically, the BRI will enable SOEs and public banks to continue to play the role of instruments of the Party, by using infrastructural projects to pursue inherently political objectives. Second, economically, OBOR represents a further consolidation of the Chinese model of state capitalism in China and its diffusion in the region. In the short term, Chinese SOEs, due to special legislative and financial support, are destined to attain substantial portions of regional markets in the sectors in which they operate. This is already discernible, looking at the role of companies such as Sino-Pec, China Mobile, and China Railways.

In the longer term, this tendency is a further step towards the logic of *guojin mintui*: namely, the consolidation of the control of the state in the strategic sectors of the Chinese political economy (Eaton 2015; Breslin and Wang 2016; Hsieh 2015). As the 2016 US–China Security and Trade Report confirmed:

> Rather than restructuring the state sector to reduce corporate debt and increase efficiency, the Chinese government continues to prop up nonviable companies with government subsidies, discounted production inputs, and favourable lending from state banks. As a result, SOEs remain the driving force behind key sectors of the Chinese economy. Under President Xi, the Chinese government has not only expanded its control over SOEs, but also exerted its influence over private companies. economically and

[2] Despite the will to preserve the size of strategic SOEs and the problem of overcapacity and decline of global demand, the government was forced to lay-off 1,8 million jobs in the state sectors only in 2016, concentrated particularly in the coal and steel industry.

> politically strategic sectors. By enhancing government oversight, centralizing bureaucratic coordination, and regulating market entry in Beijing is able to direct both private and public firms to promote state goals. (US-China Economic and Security Review Commission 2016)

This process is not free from risks. The choice of reaffirming the centrality of state ownership and consolidating the model of state capitalism has already given rise to significant costs. Incentives to moral hazard might create the premise of a structural weakness of the entire financial and productive system. As recent analyses have highlighted, the Chinese banking system is already characterized by an alarming level of nonperforming loans and other forms of structural risks (Umar and Sun 2016). Similarly, central SOEs, even if expanding in terms of capital size and market share, remain less profitable than enterprises operating in the private sectors (Berkowitz et al. 2017).

Overall, BRI represents a grandiose reaffirmation of the Chinese commitment to state capitalism and its associated power relations. This also has deep normative consequences for the regional order. Ultimately, Beijing has been promoting one of the most ambitious and extensive economic projects in history, and is doing so on the premise of ideas that reject free market capitalism, while embracing a model based on an "iron triangle" formed by public finance, SOEs and political power. This model has been already dismissed by many economists, who pointed to the structural risks associated to it and its low levels of efficiency (Huang 2008; Zheng et al. 2017). Nevertheless, the main results of the reaffirmation of the State Capitalist model are political. The BRI is likely to acquire political consensus not just for China, but for the ideas that it is promoting. In particular, the infrastructures built on the BRI agenda are likely to spread the idea that the future of the Asian economic order can be built on state-centric and "pluralist" ideas, negating the separation between state and market, political purposes and economic gains, while affirming a model of economic governance centred on state-led initiatives.

The post-Cold War globalization, until recently, led to marginalization of the role of the state in favour of the rights of the individual as "*homo oeconomicus*". Western states and international financial institutions have promoted initiatives that have increasingly enabled individuals and firms to invest, trade, and produce beyond and despite national borders, while diminishing the capacity of nation states to control capital flows, allocate investments, and develop significant industrial policies. The success of B&R might represent a sign of a possible reversal.

The success of the Chinese initiatives also scores a critical point in favour of a state capitalist economic model, and a "pluralist" and state-centric vision of the international economic order. Consequently, China reaffirms the necessity for a great power to subordinate investment decisions, credit allocation, and economic planning to the national interests. The role of the individual is subordinated to the realization of a superior, collective political objective that should be accomplished by the Chinese political community as a whole.

Beyond the consolidation of the state capitalist model, the BRI is useful for several domestic economic needs. It provides continuity with previous policies aimed at rebalancing the geographical disequilibria that emerged during the reform period, especially the growing economic and demographic imbalances between the Eastern and South Eastern Costal areas and Western and other inland areas of the country. In the 1980s, the process of economic take-off primarily involved the areas surrounding the special economic zones, that were concentrated in the coastal provinces between the Guangzhou-Shenzhen area and Shanghai. Since the 1990s, these imbalances have been reinforced by the growth of coastal cities and the influx of internal migrants. This, in turn, has generated a number of economic and political problems: from inequality, to mass migrations, to social unrest (Knight 2014).

Therefore, one of the purposes of BRI is turning provinces such as Yunnan, Sichuan, Xinjiang and Tibet into new hubs of transnational connectivity, with remote inland cities, such as Urumqi and Kunming, acquiring the role of major logistical hubs (Summers 2016). Investing in the development of more backward Western provinces is considered instrumental in addressing the so-called three evils (terrorism, extremism and separatism) in Tibet and Xinjiang, as well in alleviating the demographic pressure on the megalopolis of the South and South East, regions which continue to face enormous fluxes of internal migrants (Han and Paik 2017).[3]

[3] Infrastructural development and more in general policies aimed at rising living standards for ethnic minorities should be hardly considered a viable solution for separatism without policies aimed at allowing higher degrees of political representation and cultural and religious freedom.

Belt and Road, Geopolitics and the Regional Order

The BRI, together with the AIIB and RCEP, constitutes the main pillars of a wide geopolitical project aimed at supporting the Chinese rise both in the region and globally. On the geopolitical front, the BRI has several objectives: the expansion of the Chinese influence in the Eurasian landmass, re-orienting towards the West the centre of gravity of China's foreign policy; securing the access to sea lines of communication and transportation routes, particularly reducing the relevance of the Malacca dilemma; and securing access to energy supplies;

The necessity to re-orient China's foreign policy towards the Eurasian continent has emerged since the beginning of the 2010s and especially after the US Pivot to Asia under the Obama administration. As argued by the influential scholar Wang Jisi, in 2012, China needed to "march Westward", avoiding a direct confrontation with the US and its Asian allies, while developing new forms of cooperation with "West Asian nations, the improving the international environment and the strengthening of China's competitive abilities (Wang 2012). This strategy reflected both the necessity to reconquer some strategic space, breaking the "C-shaped encirclement ring" which the US was erecting from Japan to the South China Sea to Afghanistan (Rolland 2017, p. 116). Previously, other Chinese strategists had envisioned a westward reorientation. For instance, General Liu Yazhou, in 2001, already envisioned a "Europe-Asia land Bridge to form a greater Euro-Asian symbiotic economic belt and use the countless economic links and common interests with countries to the West in order to dismantle the U.S. encirclement of China." (Rolland 2017, p. 117).

The need to diminish the reliance on the Strait of Malacca as a main checkpoint for the Chinese shipping line is considered another fundamental geopolitical driver for the BRI. Today, some 40% of China's trade is shipped through the Strait of Malacca (UNCTAD 2016). This constitutes a fundamental strategic liability for China, since the US, in case of conflict, might easily cut the fundamental sea line of communication that connects China both with the European markets and its Middle Eastern energy supplies.

As a result, the BRI envisages several alternative routes that bypass Malacca, including the China–Pakistan Corridor. The Bangladesh–China–India–Myanmar Economic Corridor would guarantee access to the Indian Ocean, skipping the current route through the contested water of the South China Sea. The China–Mongolia–Russia corridor connecting Beijing and Ulaanbaatar with the Tran Siberian railway, as well as the New Eurasian Land Bridge Corridor linking Chongqing, Xinjiang to Eastern Europe though Kazakhstan and Belarus, would represent new land-based lines of connectivity as an alternative to existing sea-routes. Finally, the China–Central Asia–West Asia Economic Corridor could offer a new form of connection with the Middle East, securing the Chinese access to energy supplies.

Aside from strictly geopolitical aspects, the BRI embodies the Chinese will to assume regional leadership and promote its vision of the regional order and its normative foundations. The BRI, together with the AIIB and the RCEP, demonstrate how China aims to reshape the normative foundations of the regional order, promoting new forms of international cooperation, providing public goods, such as investments and infrastructures, and assuming a leadership role that it had carefully avoided in the previous decades.

Normatively, the BRI signals how the Chinese ascent entails a deep challenge to the western liberal order. The West and the US in particular, since the end of the Cold War, have advocated an evolution of the international order in a clearly solidarist direction.[4] The material primacy of the West, together with the end of the ideological competition of the Cold War, had determined a gradual evolution of the norms of sovereignty, primacy of the state over the rights of the individual, and non-interference. At the same time, economic globalization seemed to have reduced the capacity of states to regulate and direct economic forces. Nevertheless, initiatives such as the BRI testify to a partial reversal of this trend. On the one hand, the fact that China is embarking on a long-term project aimed at reshaping the region is a sign of a possible decline of the American preponderance in Asia, as well as a broader tendency towards multipolarism at the global level. On the other hand, initiatives such as the BRI signal an evolution towards forms of governments inspired to a pluralist understanding of the regional order.

The Chinese leadership has declared, on several occasions, how BRI projects would honour the norm of non-interference and the mutual respect for sovereignty (Xinhuanet 2017b). In practical terms, this enables

[4]A notable exception here is represented by the Trump administration that seems to have embraced a much more "pluralist" vision of the international order, compared with all his predecessors.

China to follow strategic and economic criteria in the allocation of resources, ignoring the regime time and or any concern for the internal situation of the countries that receive investments. Moreover, in return, China demands respect for its own sovereign and self-determination. In practice, this means avoiding criticism related to what it considers to be China's domestic affairs, including the country's human rights record, the status of Tibet and Xinjiang, as well as China's position on disputed territories.

This pluralist or sovereignist approach to global governance, which is completely detached from liberal democratic principles, represents a relevant norm both for the region and for extra-regional actors in their relationship with China. It contributes to spreading practices which willingly reject the idea that economic cooperation needs to be linked with common political values and shared norms. It has already had a very significant impact on the interactions between China and other partners. For instance, for the European Union has toned down its emphasis on human rights and democracy and accept a much more pragmatic approach to international economic governance.

A Few Bumps Ahead for the Belt and Road

The B&R Forum, held in Beijing in May 2017, offered a grandiose picture of the success of the BRI, hosting 29 foreign heads of state and government, and representatives of international organizations. Among the guests appeared key partners of the BRI, such as Russian President Putin, Pakistani President Sharif and Indonesian President Widodo. Moreover, the forum was also attended by several EU heads of government (as Italian Prime Minister Gentiloni, Spanish Prime Minister Rajoy, and French Prime Minister Raffarin,) as well as the vast majority of the leaders of ASEAN members, Secretary of the UN, Gutierrez, and the President of the World Bank, Jim Yong Kim (*The Diplomat* 2017).

The BRI Forum demonstrated how the initiative has received a positive response from a vast number of countries, giving the sense of the process of inclusion on which China has rooted its narrative for its regional blueprint (Swaine 2015). The forum also showed that many leaders and representatives of liberal democracies, as well as representatives of key international organizations, have signalled their availability to endorse a project that endorses a pluralist, state-centric approach to economic governance. In doing so, they are open to a reversal of the solidarist approach to economic governance that characterized the liberal international order in the post-Cold War era, based on a linkage between liberal norms and economic cooperation.

Despite the carefully choreographed display of the BRI Forum, the Chinese project has encountered several difficulties and pushbacks. Most of these have originated from fears of the expansion of the Chinese influence, and mistrust of China itself (Johnson 2016). The most relevant problematic states in this respect are India and Russia. Russia's reaction to the BRI project has been largely positive. In the short term, many geopolitical and economic factors have favoured a Russian positive stance on the BRI. Firstly, the aftermath of the Ukraine crisis and Western sanctions have created strong incentives for an upgrade of Sino-Russian cooperation. Moreover, Moscow hopes to link the BRI project with its own vision for a Eurasian community and connectivity, as well as its own "Pivot to Asia" (Kireeva 2017; Lagutina 2017). The improvement of bilateral relations is testified by the surge of Chinese infrastructure investments, with projects such as the Moscow–Kazan high speed railway, the first leg of a future connection between the Russian capital and Beijing, as well as an increase in the sector of raw materials (Wang 2016). China and Russia also share very similar normative orientations in terms of international order. They favour a state-centric, pluralist order, characterized by state capitalism, non-interference and sovereignty as key norms.

Nevertheless, all these improvements have failed to eliminate some deep-seated fears of the expansion of the Chinese influence in the Far East. As a result, in the longer term, the BRI could be undermined by a possible Russian opposition. The man reason is geopolitical. Russia fears the increasing asymmetry of power *vis-à-vis* Beijing. The BRI project is likely to erode the Russian influence in areas that Moscow considers to be natural spheres of influence, particularly Central Asia (Bennett 2016).

Moreover, the massive influx of Chinese investments and labourers in Russia would create an unwelcome degree of economic dependency from China, as well as a gradual takeover of the Far East provinces by Chinese nationals. In the longer term, a possible success of the BRI, coupled with an enduring isolation from the West, might generate a political subordination to Beijing that would diminish Russia's power and prestige (Kaczmarski 2015; Wishnick 2017). In this sense, Russian policymakers are wary of the historical precedent of the Cold War. The history of the Sino-Soviet alliance and the subsequent Sino-Soviet split testify to the fact that the perspective of an imbalanced Sino-Russian relationship is hardly acceptable for a state that finds itself in a weaker position (Lüthi 2010). Ultimately, today's Russia, in the same way as Mao's China, might refuse to play the role of dependent and weaker partners.

India's position on the BRI is more openly sceptical compared to Russia's. India has declined to participate in B&R. The reasons for India's opposition to BRI are primarily geopolitical. BRI is perceived as an encirclement of India, with the creation of China-dominated land and maritime trade routes. Moreover, New Delhi fears the expansion of the Chinese presence in the Indian ocean, including the fact that structures such as ports and communication routes, conceived as purely commercial, could be have a dual use (military and commercial) in the future (Pant 2017).

The second geopolitical problem, from the Indian point of view, concerns the role of Pakistan. In general, India does not have a positive view of the strengthening of the bilateral relations between Beijing and Islamabad. The BRI, and especially the China–Pakistan Economic Corridor, is considered as a threat to Indian security interests. The CPEP would bring about two very negative outcomes for New Delhi. Firstly, the corridor would cross areas of the Kashmir that are currently disputed by India and China, which would be considered a blatant violation of Indian sovereignty. Secondly, China has already started to introduce warships and submarines into the area of the deep-sea port of Gwadar, to protect its maritime hub. Indian policymakers fear that this might be the first step towards an increasingly significant Chinese military presence in a very strategic location, near the access to the Strait of Hormuz and the Persian Gulf (Jaishankar 2017). These reasons led India to defining B&R as a "national Chinese initiative driven by China's geopolitical interests", rather than a "multilateral initiative based on mutual trust" (Madan 2016).

The BRI project has also received at best a mixed reception from South Korea and Japan. During the Park Geun-hye administration, the Korean government hoped to link the BRI to its own regionalist project, the so-called Eurasian Initiative. This attempt aimed to build on the significant improvement of the bilateral relations between Beijing and Seoul from the beginning of the Park presidency and 2015 (Snyder and Byun 2017a). Since 2016, a mix of political instability in South Korea and geopolitical factors contributed to deteriorating bilateral relations. The escalation of the THAAD dispute led to the first clash between China and South Korea, in 2016. The demise of the Park government and the election of Moon Jae-in, together with the escalation of tensions between North Korea, South Korea and the US in 2017, put an end to the perspective of linking South Korean regionalist agenda with the BRI, and restricted the possibility of a Korean participation in any BRI-related activity (Snyder and Byun 2017b).

The Japanese position on the BRI somehow reverses the South Korean position. Japan perceived BRI as an unwelcome unilateral expansion of the Chinese influence. As a result, the Abe government tried to deepen bilateral relations with other countries that appeared sceptical or openly contrary to it, in particular India (Kennedy and Parker 2015). The election of Donald Trump, and the uncertainty surrounding the US role in the region, led the Abe government to a more accommodating position in 2017, when Abe himself declared that that Japan was "ready to extend cooperation", since the initiative "[had] the potential to connect East and West as well as the different regions found in between" (*Japan Times* 2017).

The states mentioned above are not the only ones that have displayed a mixed reaction to the BRI. While those in central Asia have displayed a very welcoming attitude to Chinese investments, recent analyses have argued that the expansion of the Chinese presence has corresponded with a rise in Sino-phobia among the local population, particularly in Kyrgyzstan and Kazakhstan (Pantucci and Lain 2016). The fact that China is encountering resistance of other countries that might fear the expansion of the Chinese influence it not the only potential source of strategic dilemmas for China. Others concern the relationship between the B&R project, the norms that inspire China's foreign policy, and the type of order Beijing aims to build.

In the post-Mao era, China embraced the Five Principles of Peaceful Co-Existence and in particular the principles of non-interference and respect of other states' sovereignty as guiding principles for its foreign policy. Translating these principles into practice did not appear particularly problematic for a country which, as was the case with China in the early reform era, had limited amounts of capitals overseas, or significant stakes in the development or in the political course of its neighbours.

A large-scale project such as the BRI, that will lead China to a large-scale outflow of investments and long-term economic and political commitments, is likely to put those principles under severe stress. The fundamental question here is: What will happen in case of instability or change of government, or simply a dramatic shift in terms of foreign policy in one or more of the countries that participate to the BRI? Will China continue to respect the norms of non-interference? Or, it will choose to protect its investments and, possibly, its labourers in those countries?

The BRI and the extension of the Chinese economic presence in the wide Eurasian region creates very significant incentives for a gradual shift away from the principles of non-interference, and towards a more distinctively interventionist foreign policy. In turn, this showcases the limitations of the idea of building a solidarist order, the key normative pillars of which were inspired by sovereignty and non-interference.

This dilemma is amplified by the political instability that characterizes many areas affected by the BRI. The BRI includes regions stretching throughout the so-called "arc of instability" of central Asia and the Middle East—a region in which spill-overs from conflicts in Yemen, Afghanistan and Syria might destabilize neighbouring countries with new waves of ethnic and religious violence. Together with spill-overs from existing conflicts, many of the BRI projects cross areas that are currently characterized by separatist movements. An example is the China–Pakistan economic corridor, that will cross areas in which ethnic minorities are promoting insurgencies against the national government, such as the Uyghurs in China and the Balochs in Pakistan. Moreover, the same CPEC would cross an area that is object of territorial dispute between India and Pakistan. Similarly, the planned highway connecting Kolkata and Kunming would go through areas controlled largely by the Shan and Kachin insurgencies (Djankov and Miner 2016). This would lead either to accepting the risk of serious disruption along the infrastructural networks, or to the need to insure their security, violating the principle of non-interference in other states' sovereignty.

Chinese SOEs have been instructed to apply the principle "invest locally, operate locally and integrate with the local community" to minimize anti-Chinese feelings among communities that will be interested by large projects. This aims to present infrastructural projects as opportunities for mutual cooperation rather than factors of disruption to the lives of local communities, or, worse, a reason for a surge of political and ethnic violence.

However, even though Chinese authorities and SOEs are increasingly aware of these issues, infrastructural projects might lead to negative political consequences. An example is Myanmar. The process of democratization and opening that ultimately led to the electoral triumph of

Ang San Suu Kyi and the National League for Democracy coincided with a shift away from what was perceived as excessive dependency on China. One of the factors that led Myanmar to reassess its relationship with China was the planned construction of a large dam on the Irrawaddy river. The works for the damn led to great costs for Myanmar, in terms of relocation of population into areas that have been affected by ethnic insurgency for more than four decades. The government of Myanmar decided to stop the project, generating a significant economic loss for the Chinese firms involved. This opened a rift between the countries that created incentives for the Burmese regime to "pivot" to the West and start a process of political opening (Huang 2015; Jones 2014).

This is an example of how forms of cooperation that are presented as "win-win" and "harmonious" by the Chinese government can trigger an unpredictable chain of events and generate significant political problems. In this case, Beijing accepted the economic loss and respected Myanmar's self-determination, even if it led to a rapprochement with the West. In the future, in case of higher losses in terms of capital and political interests, China might decide to abandon the principle of non-intervention and reassert its influence.

Conclusion

The BRI is surely the most "eye-catching" initiative among the three analysed here (Ferdinand 2016). It is also the initiative that is likely to have the most direct impact on the process of contestation and renegotiation of key primary institutions of the regional order in Asia. This chapter has made revealed the BRI involves an attempt to renegotiate the geographic boundaries of the region. In this case, it involves both norms and institutions: namely, the "social" dimension of the region, as well as a more distinctively material dimension, since China is trying to physically redesign the patterns of connectivity through the creation of a new network of infrastructures.

The BRI is the most tangible manifestation of a geopolitical re-orientation of Chinese foreign policy, which assigns a renewed relevance to the relations with continental Asia, and, above all, to the creation of forms of connectivity linking China to Europe. This completes a long-term evolution in the relationship between China and the Asian regional order. During the Deng and Jiang periods, China broke the previous isolation. During the Hu period, it concentrated its efforts on the creation of East Asian forms of regionalism. Finally, under Xi, China has proposed itself as a centre of a vast region, spanning from Central Asia to the South and East China Sea, completing a long process of a return to the centre of the region. This process of reorientation is also associated with the neo-Confucian elements of the current Chinese narrative, which present Beijing's renewed centrality as a foundation for a future "harmonious order".

Renegotiating the boundaries of the region in this case also has crucial strategic implications: the effort to downgrade the Malacca Strait as a necessary bottleneck for trade and maritime connections between Asia, the Middle East and Europe. In turn, this attempt effects the long-term objective of diminishing the Chinese vulnerability in case of a further escalation in the competition for influence and security with the US.

The B&R also has important consequence in terms of sovereignty. BRI reflects a clearly pluralist and sovereignist orientation. Through BRI, China has reaffirmed the centrality of the mutual respect of sovereignty and non-interference as fundamental norms that inspire its foreign policy. The chapter has explored both the relationship between post-colonial ideas that helped legitimize the current Chinese foreign policy course and the practice of these principles, and how these principles serve the country's interests.

Adhering to, and practicing, the principle of non-interference represents an essential point for China for several reasons. Since beginning of the reform and opening era has presented itself as different from the other great powers of the past. The widespread use of a post-colonial narrative has led China to reject forms of intervention in the domestic politics of other states as a form of imperialism from which it would prefer to refrain, by virtue of its own experience of country that has suffered the humiliation of being colonized (Dian 2017). Consequently, significant deviations from the principle of non-interference would significantly damage the idea that China is different from "Western Imperialists", and uniquely equipped to understand and promote the interests of developing Asian countries.

Promoting forms of "sovereignist" regional governance has other advantages, from the Chinese standpoint. It allows the promotion of forms of economic cooperation that are not subordinated to the domestic regime of the partners or their standards, in terms of rule of law and human rights. While this aspect is in continuity with the past Chinese foreign policy, the scale of BRI makes it a significant development in terms of regional and even global order. Since the end of the Cold War, Western states have tried to promote a systematic linkage between rule of law, democracy promotion and economic cooperation (Clark 2005; Slaughter 2004). However, China's initiatives contest this principle, which is in turn denounced as a form of "imperialist intrusion" of the West.

The chapter has also highlighted the inherent tension between the pluralist and sovereignist design promoted through the BRI and the likely unintended consequences that the project might generate. BRI is a grandiose plan that will lead to the increase of China's economic, social and political presence throughout the Eurasian continent and beyond. This will create significant incentives to abandon the principle of non-interference in other states sovereignty.

B&R infrastructure projects will involve some of the most unstable regions of the continent and lead to the creation of strategically located connectivity hubs, such as the deep-sea port of Gwadar. In case of unfavourable political developments, it would be difficult for the Chinese policymakers to continue to adhere to the principle of respect of other state's sovereignty. Possible examples are local ethnic or religious conflicts and insurgencies that might lead to a Chinese direct or indirect intervention. Another main reason why China might reconsider its approach is the need to proactively protect its strategic assets along the Silk Roads, as testified by the deployment of the Chinese Navy near Gwadar. This possibility has been already perceived by neighbouring countries as threatening, in terms of a fear of the expansion of Chinese influence.

The other significant way in which BRI leads to a process of contestation and renegotiation of the regional order concerns the market as a primary institution. BRI can also be interpreted as the continuation of a strategy aimed at preserving the role of Chinese SOEs both cornerstone of the export driven, investment intensive model that has characterized China in the reform era. BRI will address the problem of overconsumption that has plagued the Chinese state industries, while favouring the process of consolidation of key national champions. Here, it is important to underline two key features of the Chinese state capitalism in relation to the market as the primary institution. The first is the distortive effect on international markets determined by the fact that Chinese SOEs, being subject to special fiscal and financial treatment, tend to prevail over private firms. Perhaps, most importantly, Chinese SOEs retain a relevant political value, since they can be used as instruments to implement China's interests by Chinese policymakers. Finally, BRI will contribute to lock in the power structure that presides over the role of the SOE, namely the "iron triangle", formed by the Party, public banks, and SOEs.

Even if China, does not aim to export its own model, the diffusion of practices associated with state capitalism in the wider region is significant. The most direct effect is the promotion of a model of development based on the central role of heavy industry and infrastructure, sectors in which large enterprises and the state play a decisive role. Even more importantly, BRI, from this point of view, constitutes an important development towards the consolidation of pluralist economic order, in which the role of firms and economic agents is subordinated to political power and national interests.

Finally, BRI also entails a process of the revision of great power management as a primary institution. BRI is one of the most visible manifestations of China's ascent to great power status, which in turn is increasingly recognized by a number of regional and extra-regional partners. It expresses a synthesis of ideological elaboration, strategic planning, and mobilization of economic and social resources. The Chinese quest to occupy a position of leadership in the region is surely related to its fate, that of whether it will be successful or if the obstacles along its way will prove too high (Fig. 4.1).

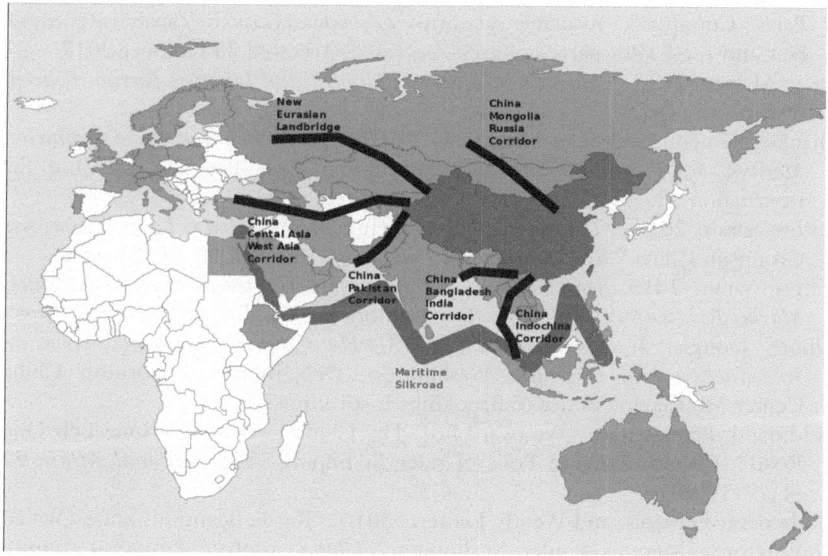

Fig. 4.1 The figure shows the six main corridors and the Maritime Silk Road that define the Belt and Road Iniatiative

Bibliography

Bennett, Mia M. 2016. "The Silk Road Goes North: Russia's Role within China's Belt and Road Initiative." *Area Development and Policy* 1 (3): 341–351.

Berkowitz, Daniel, Hong Ma, and Shuichiro Nishioka. 2017. "Recasting the Iron Rice Bowl: The Reform of China's State Owned Enterprises." *Review of Economics and Statistics*. On line first version.

Breslin, Shaun. 2010. "Government-Industry Relations in China: A Review of the Art of the State." CSGR Working Paper 272/10.

Breslin, Shaun, and Zhengyi Wang. 2016. "Governing the Chinese Market." Paper Presented at the ISA Conference Atlanta.

Cai, Fang, Albert Park, Yaohui Zhao, Loren Brandt, and Thomas Rawski, eds. 2008. *China's Great Economic Transformation*. Cambridge: Cambridge University Press.

Callahan, William A. 2016. "China's Belt and Road Initiative and the New Eurasian Order." Oslo: Norwegian Institute of International Affairs, Policy Brief.

Clark, Ian. 2005. *Legitimacy in International Society*. Oxford: Oxford University Press.

CSIS Reconnecting Asia. 2017, October 26. "Belt and Road at China's 19th Party Congress". Available at https://reconasia.csis.org/analysis/entries/belt-and-road-19th-party-congress/accessed. Accessed 28 October 2017.

Dian, Matteo. 2017. *Contested Memories in Chinese and Japanese Foreign Policies*. Oxford: Elsevier.

Djankov, Simeon, and Sean Miner, eds. 2016. *China's Belt and Road Initiative: Motives, Scope, and Challenges*. Washington, DC: Peterson Institute for International Economics.

Eaton, Sarah. 2013. "The Gradual Encroachment of an Idea: Large Enterprise Groups in China." *The Copenhagen Journal of Asian Studies* 31 (2): 5–22.

Eaton, Sarah. 2015. *The Advance of the State in Contemporary China: State-Market Relations in the Reform Era*. Cambridge: Cambridge University Press.

Elliott, Douglas J., and Kai Yan. 2013. *The Chinese Financial System an Introduction and Overview*. Washington, DC: John L. Thornton China Center Monograph Series 6. Brookings Institutions.

Ferdinand, Peter. 2016. "Westward ho—The China Dream and "One Belt One Road": Chinese Foreign Policy Under Xi Jinping." *International Affairs* 92 (4): 941–957.

Godement, François, and Wendy Leutert. 2016. "Big Is Beautiful? State-Owned Enterprise Mergers Under Xi Jinping." *China Analysis. European Council of Foreign Relations*. Available at http://www.ecfr.eu/page/-/China_Analysis_%E2%80%93_Big_is_Beautiful.pdf. Accessed 26 September 2016.

Han, Enze, and Christopher Paik. 2017. "Ethnic Integration and Development in China." *World Development* 93 (3): 31–42.

Heilmann, Sebastian, and Lea Shih. 2013. "The Rise of Industrial Policy in China." Harvard-Yenching Institute Working Paper Series. Available at https://www.harvard-yenching.org/sites/harvard-yenching.org/files/featurefiles/Sebastian%20Heilmann%20and%20Lea%20Shih_The%20Rise%20of%20Industrial%20Policy%20in%20China%201978-2012.pdf. Accessed 26 September 2017.

Hsieh, Chiang Tia. 2015. *Grasp the Large, Let Go of the Small: The Transformation of the State Sector in China*. Washington, DC: Brookings Papers on Economic Activity.

Hsieh, Chang-Tai, and Zheng Michael Song. 2015. *Grasp the Large, Let Go of the Small: The Transformation of the State Sector in China*. National Bureau of Economic Research, 1.

Huang, Chiung Chiu. 2015. "Balance of Relationship: The Essence of Myanmar's China Policy." *The Pacific Review* 28 (2): 89–210.

Huang, Yasheng. 2008. *Capitalism with Chinese Characteristics: Entrepreneurship and the State*. Cambridge: Cambridge University Press.

Jaishankar, Dhruva. 2017, August 21. "India Feeling the Heat on Belt and Road." *The Interpreter*. Available at https://www.lowyinstitute.org/the-interpreter/india-feeling-heat-belt-road. Accessed 14 September.

Jakobson, Linda, and Manuel Ryan. 2016. "How Are Foreign Policy Decisions Made in China?" *Asia & The Pacific Policy Studies* 3 (1): 101–110.

Japan Times. 2017, June 24. "Japan and One Belt, One Road." Available at https://www.japantimes.co.jp/opinion/2017/06/24/editorials/japan-one-belt-one-road/#.WcoWt8gjFPY. Accessed 19 September 2017.

Johnson, Christopher K. 2016. *President Xi Jinping's "Belt and Road" Initiative A Practical Assessment of the Chinese Communist Party's Roadmap for China's Global Resurgence*. Washington, DC: Center for Strategic and International Studies.

Jones, Lee. 2014. "Explaining Myanmar's Regime Transition: The Periphery is Central." *Democratization* 21 (5): 780–802.

Kaczmarski, Marcin. 2015. *Russia-China Relations in the Post-crisis International Order*. London: Routledge.

Kallio, Jyrki. 2016. "China New Foreign Politics. Xi Jinping's Universal Rule by Virtue." Finnish Institute for International Affairs Policy Brief 189.

Kennedy, Scott, and David A. Parker. 2015. *Building China's One Belt One Road*. Washington, DC: Center for Strategic International Studies. Available at https://www.csis.org/analysis/building-china%E2%80%99s-%E2%80%9Cone-belt-one-road%E2%80%9D. Accessed 19 September 2017.

Kireeva, Anna. 2017. *Positive Scenario I*. Seoul: ASAN Institute for Policy Studies. http://www.theasanforum.org/category/alternative-scenarios/?post_id=8244.

Knight, John. 2014. "Economic Causes and Cures of Social Instability in China." *China & World Economy* 22 (2): 5–21.

Lagutina, Maria. 2017. "Improving Relations with Russia and Ukraine." In *China's Belt and Road: A Game Changer?* edited by Alessia Amighini, 53–74. Milan: Istituto per gli Studi di Politica Internazionale.

Lardy, Nicholas R. 2012. *Sustaining China's Economic Growth after the Financial Crisis.* Washington, DC: Peterson Institute for International Economics.

Leutert, Wendy. 2016. "Challenges Ahead in China's Reform of State-Owned Enterprises." *Asia Policy* 21 (1): 88–118.

Liu, Ye. 2014. "Interprovincial Migration, Regional Development and State Policy in China, 1985–2010." *Applied Spatial Analysis and Policy* 7 (1): 47–70.

Lüthi, Lorenz M. 2010. *The Sino-Soviet Split: Cold War in the Communist World.* Princeton, NJ: Princeton University Press.

Madan, Tanvi. 2016, March 14. "What India Thinks about China's One Belt, One Road Initiative (but Does't Explicitly Say)." Brooking Institution. Available at https://www.brookings.edu/blog/order-from-chaos/2016/03/14/what-india-thinks-about-chinas-one-belt-one-road-initiative-but-doesnt-explicitly-say/. Accessed 14 June 2017.

Naughton, Barry. 2015. "The Transformation of the State Sector: SASAC, the Market Economy, and the New National Champions." In *State Capitalism, Institutional Adaptation, and the Chinese Miracle*, edited by Barry Naughton and Kellee S. Tsai, 46–71. Cambridge: Cambridge University Press.

Naughton, Barry. 2016a. "State Enterprise Reform: Missing in Action." *China Economic Quarterly* 20 (2): 15–22.

Naughton, Barry. 2016b. "Two Trains Running: Supply-Side Reform, SOE Reform and the Authoritative Personage." *China Leadership Monitor* 50 (19): 1949–2008.

Pant, Harsh V. 2017, June 22. "India Challenges Intentions on One Belt, One Road Initiative." *Yale Global On Line.* Available at http://yaleglobal.yale.edu/content/india-challenges-chinas-intentions-one-belt-one-road-initiative Accessed 22 September 2017.

Pantucci, Raffaello, and Sarah Lain. 2016. "IV. Perception Problems of the Belt and Road Initiative from Central Asia." *Whitehall Papers* 88 (1): 47–55.

Pearson, Magaret M. 2015. "State Owned Business and Party—State Regulation in China's Modern Political Economy." In *State Capitalism, Institutional Adaptation, and the Chinese Miracle*, edited by Barry Naughton and Kellee S. Tsai, 27–45. Cambridge: Cambridge University Press.

Peck, Jamie, and Jun Zhang. 2013. "A Variety of Capitalism… with Chinese Characteristics?" *Journal of Economic Geography* 13 (3): 357–396.

Rolland, Nadège. 2017. *China's Eurasian Century? Political and Strategic Implications of the Belt and Road Initiative.* Washington, DC: The National Bureau of East Asia Research.

Ruan, Zongze. 2017. *Belt and Road Initiative: A New Frontier for Win-Win Cooperation*. Beijing: China Institute for International Studies. http://www.ciis.org.cn/english/2017-07/21/content_39050638.htm.

Shambaugh, David. 2013. *China Goes Global. The Partial Power*. Oxford: Oxford University Press.

Shen, Guagjun, and Binkai Chen. 2017. "Zombie Firms and Over-Capacity in Chinese Manufacturing." *China Economic Review* 44 (1): 327–342.

Slaughter, Anne-Marie. 2004. *A New World Order*. Princeton, NJ: Princeton University Press.

Snyder, Scott, and See-Won Byun. 2017a. "North Korea, THAAD Overshadow Beijing and Seoul's 25th Anniversary." *Comparative Connections: A Triannual E-Journal on East Asian Bilateral Relations* 19 (2): 81–90.

Snyder, Scott, and See-Won Byun. 2017b. "South Korea's Diplomatic Triangle." *Comparative Connections: A Triannual E-Journal on East Asian Bilateral Relations* 17 (1): 1–10.

Summers, Tim. 2016. "China's 'New Silk Roads': Sub-national Regions and Networks of Global Political Economy." *Third World Quarterly* 37 (9): 1628–1643.

Swaine, Michael D. 2015. "Chinese Views and Commentary on the "One Belt, One Road" Initiative." *China Leadership Monitor* 47 (2): 1–24.

The Diplomat. 2017, May 12. "Belt and Road Attendees List." http://thediplomat.com/2017/05/belt-and-road-attendees-list/. Accessed 25 September 2017.

Umar, Mohammad, and Gang Sun. 2016. "Non-performing Loans (NPLs), Liquidity Creation, and Moral Hazard: Case of Chinese Banks." *China Finance and Economic Review* 4 (1): 1–23.

United Nations Conference on Trade and Development. 2016. *Review of Maritime Transport 2016*. New York, NY: United Nations Publication. http://unctad.org/en/PublicationsLibrary/rmt2016_en.pdf.

United Nations Conference on Trade and Development. 2017. *Trade and Development Report 2017. Beyond Austerity: Towards a Global New Deal*. New York, NY: United Nations Publication. http://unctad.org/en/PublicationsLibrary/tdr2017_en.pdf.

US-China Economic and Security Review Commission. 2011. *Going Out: An Overview of China's Outward Foreign Direct Investment*. Washington, DC: USCC Research Report.

US-China Economic and Security Review Commission. 2016. *2016 Report to Congress*. Washington, DC.

Wang, Jisi. 2012. *"Marching Westwards": The Rebalancing of China's Geostrategy*. Beijing: Center for International and Strategic Studies, Peking University, Report.

Wang, Tao. 2016, September 30. "The Great Russia-China Oil Alliance Is Here (and Why It Matters)." *The National Interest*, 2016. Available at http://nationalinterest.org/blog/the-buzz/the-great-russia-china-oil-alliance-here-why-it-matters-17883. Accessed 12 September 2017.

Wildau, Gabriel. 2017, July 9. "China Prepares Fresh Round of State Orchestrated Mega-Mergers." *Financial Times*. https://www.ft.com/content/e3972f54-62e2-11e7-91a7-502f7ee26895.

Wishnick, Elizabeth. 2017. "In Search of the 'Other' in Asia: Russia–China Relations Revisited." *The Pacific Review* 30 (1): 114–132.

Wong, Christine. 2011. "The Fiscal Stimulus Program and Problems of Macroeconomic Management in China." 32nd Annual Meeting of OECD Senior Budget Officials Luxembourg, 6–7 June. Public Governance and Territorial Development Directorate Public Governance Committee.

Wu, Gang. 2017, October 2. "SOEs Lead Infrastructure Push in 1,700 'Belt and Road' Projects." *Caixing Global*. http://www.caixinglobal.com/2017-05-10/101088332.html. Accessed 2 October 2017.

Xinhuanet. 2017a, March 23. "The Belt and Road Will Help Countries to Develop." http://news.xinhuanet.com/fortune/2017-03/23/c_129516876.htm.

Xinhuanet. 2017b, May 14. "Full Text of President Xi's Speech at Opening of Belt and Road Forum." http://news.xinhuanet.com/english/2017-05/14/c_136282982.htm. Accessed 23 September 2017.

Yu, Jie. 2017. "China's One Belt One Road: A Reality Check." LDE IDEAS Strategic Update. https://medium.com/@lseideas/chinas-one-belt-one-road-a-reality-check-b28030ac6d3b.

Zhang, Feng. 2016. "China as a Global Force." *Asia & the Pacific Policy Studies* 3 (1): 120–128.

Zheng, Kevin, Gerald Yong Gao, and Hongxin Zhao. 2017. "State Ownership and Firm Innovation in China: An Integrated View of Institutional and Efficiency Logics." *Administrative Science Quarterly* 62 (2): 375–404.

Zhong, Nan. 2017, May 9. "SOEs to Take Lead Role along Belt and Road." *China Daily*. http://www.chinadaily.com.cn/business/2017-05/09/content_29258516.htm. Accessed 2 October 2017.

CHAPTER 5

The Regional Comprehensive Economic Partnership (RCEP)

Abstract This chapter locates the Regional Comprehensive Economic Partnership (RCEP) within the wider Chinese blueprint for regional governance in Asia. It highlights how the agreement, especially after the American abandonment of Trans-Pacific Partnership (TPP), become functional to the Chinese image of potential regional leader and key supporter of free trade and economic globalization. The chapter looks at the likely content of the agreement underlying how key provisions of the RCEP will be represent a compromise between the objective of promoting China's centrality in the region, the need to overcome non-tariff barriers to trade, and the necessity to promote Beijing's interests and normative orientation. The chapter underlines how the RCEP will particularly protect the Chinese capacity to use State-Owned Enterprises (SOEs) as instrument of economic and political influence.

Keywords Trade · Rules of origin · Non tariff barriers · ASEAN+6
State owned entreprises · Regional order

The Origin and the Changing Purpose of the RCEP

The Regional Comprehensive Economic Partnership (RCEP) is a FTA currently under negotiation among the ASEAN+6 countries: on the one hand, Brunei, Myanmar, Cambodia, Malaysia, Philippines, Singapore, Thailand and Vietnam (ASEAN); on the other, China,

M. Dian and S. Menegazzi, *New Regional Initiatives in China's Foreign Policy*, https://doi.org/10.1007/978-3-319-75505-2_5

Japan, South Korea, Australia, New Zealand and India (+6 countries). All these states taken together have more than 3 billion citizens and more than 40% of global trade.

The RCEP in this conception was not a Chinese initiative. The ASEAN+6 framework is an evolution of earlier ideas based on the ASEAN+3 template promoted by the East Asia Vision Group (EAVG) between 2001 and 2004. The initiative was announced during the 19th ASEAN Summit in Bali, Indonesia, from November 2011 and then formally launched at the 20th ASEAN Summit in Cambodia, in November 2012. In 2012, ASEAN had completed ASEAN+1 free trade agreements (FTAs) with China, Japan, Australia, New Zealand, India and South Korea. This template reaffirmed the ASEAN centrality and the ASEAN way, at the time challenged by the Trans-Pacific Partnership (TPP), which had created a rift in the organization, dividing states leaning towards China and those oriented to welcome the US rebalancing to Asia (Fukunaga and Isono 2013).

ASEAN+1 agreements were negotiated at different points in time and contained different norms and principles. The proliferation of FTAs and other types of agreement has led to the so-called "noodle bowl" phenomenon (Dent 2013; Emmers and Ravenhill 2011). ASEAN-centred and the majority of Asian bilateral FTAs are primarily focused on the liberalization of goods. Consequently, they created several different standards in sectors that generate non-tariff barriers to trade, such as rules of origin (ROOs), investment protection, and competition. The proliferation of agreements and the persistence to non-tariff barriers led to both to the fragmentation of the trade system, and to a minimal impact of agreements in terms of actual trade flows. The noodle bowl has been recognized as a source of economic, legal, and political problems both by Asian political elites and by the scholarly community (Bhagwati 2008). Consequently, it was recognized that to increase the volume of trade in goods and services. Asian economies had to find a way to disentangle the noodle bowl, creating a multilateral agreement aimed at harmonizing the different pre-existing standards.

With the emergence of the other two key initiatives of the Chinese regional project, the BRI and the AIIB, the role of the RCEP evolved significantly. The RCEP started to be considered as part of a contest of templates between a Chinese-led multilateral agreement, rooted in the Chinese leadership and norms, and a Trans-Pacific template promoted by the US.

The TPP represented the cornerstone of the trans-pacific economic regionalism promoted by the Obama administration under the rubric of the Pivot to Asia. Crucially, it was aimed at infusing the regional economic order with solidarist elements. With solidarist, we refer here to elements of "economic solidarism". In this sense, TPP aimed at enforcing the rights of individuals and firms to freely operate with a region, without preferential treatment or direct state intervention in the economy (Dian 2017). This appeared in direct opposition to China's vision of a pluralist regional order, in which the need to solve the problem of the noodle bowl was balanced by a normative aversion for intrusive "behind the borders"[1] forms of economic governance. In this context, the RCEP represented an economic and political alternative, rooted in a different membership, with radical and contrasting approaches to trade and economic integration.

The US withdrawal from the TPP in early 2017 determined a further evolution in the role of the RCEP. Rather than one of the many alternative solutions to achieve a comprehensive economic and commercial integration in Asia, it suddenly became the only significant agreement with the potential to generate a substantial acceleration of economic integration in the region. This offered China a valuable opportunity to shape the regional economic order according to its preferences and its ideas.

This chapter shows how the RCEP aims at promoting an Asian template for economic and commercial integration, while advancing a model of economic integration, favourable to China's norms and interests, within the limits of a pluralist understanding of the regional order. In contrast with TPP, or other so-called "gold standard" free trade pacts, Chinese proposals on trade try to minimize the intrusive aspects of economic integration, limiting the role of binding chapters on non-tariff barriers. Moreover, it will not impose high standards in terms of workers' rights, environmental protection and financial transparency. Finally, the RCEP is compatible with a "state capitalist" orientation that allows a prominent role for state owned enterprises.

[1]Behind the border regulations refers to the need to harmonize domestic regulatory standards to lower non-tariff barriers to trade. Generally promoting, monitoring and enforcing common regulatory standards in entails accepting forms of governance that erode the national economic sovereignty, limiting a state's capacity to decide on several rules and regulations.

Economic Integration and the Chinese Narrative

Before entering into details of the likely content of the agreement and the likely consequences for economic and political dynamics in East Asia, it is important to discuss how an apparently technical agreement such as the RCEP fits into the contemporary Chinese narrative on regional and global governance. The RCEP does not occupy a place equivalent to B&R, or even the AIIB in the contemporary Chinese discourse. However, Xi and other leaders have often included references to trade and economic governance when describing China's attempt to promote a new economic order in Asia and beyond. As a result, it is worth underlining how Beijing's approach to trade reflects the central themes we explored in this volume: the necessity of including the non-Western world in global governance; the need of the establishing of a "new type of international organizations"; China's will and capacity to generate a "harmonious order"; and respect for the political and social differences among states. These themes are broadly connected with the two intellectual traditions that we labelled post-colonial nationalism and neo-Confucianism.

China is described as ready to assume the responsibility of promoting globalization and the economic integration, while advancing the interest of the entire international community. Ultimately, it would reassume its position of regional leadership not to impose a form of economic hegemony, but rather to build a harmonious economic order, in which diversity of interest and identity can coexist and prosper. As such, in being active in promoting the RCEP, the Chinese Ministry of Commerce has stressed, on several occasions, that China will continue to play a constructive role in the negotiations, in order to support ASEAN's leading and central role in the agreement (Chinese Ministry of Commerce 2017).

It is important to underline that last year, especially after the election of Donald Trump, and with the following withdrawal of the US from TPP negotiations, these themes were supplemented by other significant elements: the fact the international order is experiencing a leadership crisis and the idea that China is today the main upholder of economic globalization. From this point of view, populism, protectionism, lack of leadership and incapacity to govern the forces of globalization are considered symptoms of the malaise of the West. Consequently, China is presented as ready to assume a leadership role regionally and, in the foreseeable future, also globally.

It is important to note that this discourse also includes an implicit argument against liberal democracy. From a neo-Confucian perspective, the rise of populism and the protectionist turn looming large over the US and Europe, is also caused by the alleged incapacity of contemporary democracy to act according to the long-term interests of the global community. From this perspective, assigning priority to a short-term popular will over merit and competence has led the West to undermine its capacity to guide contemporary economic globalization (Ford 2015; Bell 2016).

These themes emerged in Xi Jinping's speech at the 2017 World Economic Forum in Davos. This speech clearly articulated the first explicit bid for leadership in the current international economic order, and one of the strongest call for free trade and globalization from the Chinese leadership so far. Xi firstly declared openly that contemporary economic globalization is an indisputable fact that cannot be refused. He then criticized the US and the EU for trying to hide from this reality and retreating from any attempt to promote new and more advanced forms of global governance. In line with the tradition of Chinese post-colonialism, Xi stressed the need for inclusion and representation of developing countries and especially Asian countries, creating alternative forms of government or reforming the existing ones. He stated:

> the global governance system has not embraced those new changes and is therefore inadequate in terms of representation and inclusiveness. The global industrial landscape is changing and new industrial chains, value chains and supply chains are taking shape. However, trade and investment rules have not kept pace with these developments, resulting in acute problems such as closed mechanisms and fragmentation of rules. (World Economic Forum 2017)

Moreover, consistent the tradition originating with the Five Principles of Peaceful Co-existence, he stressed how economic governance should maintain the respect of local conditions, autonomous paths to development, and avoiding infringing states' sovereignty and national conditions. As he argued:

> [We should] proceed from our respective national conditions and embark on the right pathway of integrating into economic globalization with the right pace. We should strike a balance between efficiency and equity to ensure that different countries, different social strata and different groups of people all share in the benefits of economic globalization. (ibid.)

Together with these post-colonial and developmentalist ideas, the narrative proposed by the current leadership on trade and economic globalization is also increasingly infused of by neo-Confucian ideas. For instance, the same Davos speech, possibly the strongest Chinese defence of free trade and globalization in recent years, is clearly inspired by neo-Confucian ideas proposed by philosopher such as Zhao Tingyang or IR theorists such as Yan Xuetong. For instance, Xi argued:

> we should pursue a well-coordinated and inter-connected approach to develop a model of open and win-win cooperation. Today, mankind has become a close-knit community of shared future. (ibid.)

Here, it is important to connect the neo-Confucian ideal background, the Chinese narrative and policy proposals. Here Xi paints the picture of the Chinese capacity to guide Asia towards a new harmonious order in which economic development, connectivity and respect of the differences would gradually diffuse political conflicts. Neo-Confucian ideas contribute to legitimizing China's opening to the world and to global capitalism, as well as its attempt to produce an allegedly more just, but also more stable, international order. Within this narrative, the leadership and the centrality of China in Asia and in the dynamics of contemporary globalization are described as an opportunity rather than a threat for other countries. The neo-Confucian ideals help to smooth the contradiction between equality and mutually beneficious interaction and a progressively more evident leadership role for Beijing, as an engine of regional economic development, as well as political guidance for regional governance.

Defining China as the ultimate defender of economic globalization and free trade is a crucial part of Beijing's attempt to contest the international hierarchy on which the global and international order is based. The Trump administration, with its protectionist policies and its "America first" rhetoric, has opened an unexpected window of opportunity for China, which can present itself as a responsible, inclusive, and forward-looking leader in the making, in contrast with a declining, irresponsible and inward-looking US. The perception that Washington is working to degrade the current international economic order, refusing to make progress on new agreements, and even trying to renegotiate existing ones, has made Asian partners much more receptive to the Chinese calls for free trade and an open and inclusive economic system.

Even if China has proclaimed itself as the defender of economic globalization, the norms and the values on which its regional initiatives are based are rooted in a unique understanding of rule and norms on which the regional and global economic order should based, particularly when it comes to relations between state and market and economics and politics. The following section will explain how the RCEP represent a valuable instrument to promote forms of commercial integration coherent with Beijing's principles and interests.

At the same time, the narrative is functional to China's economic interests. It is representative of a specific political tradition, which tends to combine the idea of China's development as possible only through harmony and win-win strategies, i.e., Chinese development, combined with the prosperity of its neighbour countries. Therefore, according to Zhang Jianping, China's decision to support the RCEP is the result of a series of highly strategic considerations. First, it is the need to implement its "external opening strategy" (外开放战略 *wai kaifang zhanlue*), that is, China envisioning the internationalization strategy of its industry and firms. Second, it is the fact that participation in RCEP negotiations allows China to adjust its economic structure in line with the rules and practices of the global economy. Third, the RCEP represents the most valid alternative to a US-led economic order, therefore a valid instrument to counter-balance the American hegemony in the Asia-Pacific region (Zhang 2014). Not surprisingly, in the Chinese literature, academic discussions about the RCEP are often framed within a discourse that tends to compare the Asian project with the TPP negotiations. Here, the narrative is also clear: since the TPP was drafted in October 2015, the economic cooperation and integration process in the Asia-Pacific has become more complex. Due to China's exclusion, the agreement is perceived as an ad hoc strategy to contain Chinese economic growth in the Asia-Pacific in parallel with the intent to implement the US supremacy in the region (Zou and Wu 2016).

The Content of the Regional Comprehensive Economic Partnership (RCEP)

RCEP is currently still under negotiation, therefore we cannot provide a comprehensive analysis of the content of the agreement. At the time of writing, 19 negotiating rounds have been held. Member states have indicated 2018 as a desired date for the completion of the agreement, but there is no clear sign that that the end of the negotiations is in sight. However, at this stage, relying both on leaked documents on the negotiations, official statements, and scholarly analyses, it is possible to describe the likely content of the agreement. Moreover, we will connect key ideas underpinning the Chinese approach to trade negotiations, the likely content of some of the key chapters, and their impact on the process of contestation of the regional economic order.

During the November 2012 Summit in Bali, the leaders of ASEAN+6 approved the guiding principles, which define eight negotiation areas: trade in goods; trade in services; investment; economic and technical cooperation; intellectual property (IP); competition; and dispute settlement. It was also decided that the RCEP was not aimed at substituting the existing agreements that would remain in force. On the contrary, the RCEP would lead to a reorganization of the rule and a harmonization of the standards. On 9–13 May 2013, the first meeting of the Trade Negotiating Committee held in Brunei saw officials from the 16 governments participating in the negotiations to set up the goals upon which the RCEP discussions would be conducted, respectively: to establish an open trade and investment environment in the region in order to facilitate the growth and expansion of regional trade; and to boost economic development to strengthen economic cooperation, building on existing economic networks in the region (ASEAN 2016).

From this early phase of the negotiations, it emerged that, on the one hand, the RCEP was responding to an economic and legal need: namely, the necessity to harmonize standards and norms, in order to make the institutional structure of free trade in Asia more efficient. On the other hand, this necessity offered the possibility to shape the normative boundaries of the regional economic order.

With the progress of negotiations, China has gradually assumed a more prominent role in the negotiating rounds, starting to consider the RCEP both as a fundamental component of the emerging Chinese blueprint for the region, and a necessary alternative to the model of economic integration promoted by the Obama administration though the TPP (Panda 2014; Wilson 2015).

TPP negotiators pursued the idea of reaching a "gold standard" and "WTO Plus" agreement (Dai 2015). The TPP imposed high regulatory standards for countries with different levels of economic development and very different economic and productive structures.

This was considered necessary by the supporters and the negotiators of the agreement to effectively "level the playing field" and build a real free trade area in the Pacific Basin (Elms 2013).

In general terms, the RCEP is less ambitious than TPP in terms of regulatory depth. The promoters of the RCEP generally aim to reach a "WTO consistent" agreement, rather than "WTO plus". The RCEP embraces the idea that the agreement should reflect distinct levels of development of participating economies, allowing special and differential treatment for lesser-developed economies. For instance, unlike the TPP, the RCEP does not have any labour or environmental protection provisions. Therefore, it is more attractive to some ASEAN countries, while reducing the complexities of negotiations. In addition, the RCEP represents a key opportunity for smaller members that are part of the agreement, allowing them easy access to the larger consumer market (Freddie 2017).

This approach to trade negotiations is coherent with the main ideas underpinning China's regionalist project and more generally contemporary Chinese foreign policy. The RCEP can in fact can be described as another example of a "new type of international organization", in which China seeks to establish win-win, mutually beneficial relations, respecting the differences in terms of values or political regimes. Moreover, the Chinese government has stated that the RCEP represents another attempt to promote new forms of inclusion and a better representation of the voices and the interests of developing countries. Consequently, the Ministry of Commerce of the PRC has stated that the agreement will contribute to rewriting economic rules in Asia:

> The RCEP contributes to the formulation of the rule systems that accord with the development interests of East Asia… (the RCEP) is conducive to forming rule systems that accord with the development of Asia in more sectors, so to increase the voice in the new round of international rules game. (Ministry of Commerce of the PRC 2014)

The RCEP agreement, as with other trade deals of the new generation, will include a considerable number of chapters. The most significant are: ROOs, investments, competition, dispute resolution mechanisms, competition, and services.

These topics are crucial because they will define the relationship between the agreement itself and the normative foundation of regional economic order, especially when it comes to the delicate balance between the economic need for harmonization and coordination, and the political will to preserve a pluralist economic order, rooted in member states' economic sovereignty.

ROOs are a key feature of any FTA . According to the literature on the subject, the establishment of common ROOs is necessary for transforming the network of overlapping FTAs, connecting ASEAN, Japan and China into an effective multilateral trade agreement (Estevadeordal et al. 2009).[2] Negotiators can choose between two models: the "cut and sew" model or the more restrictive "yarn forward model". The latter, which was used in the TPP, leads to the exclusion of products from preferential trade that are simply assembled in a member country, since, to be eligible for preferential trade, a product should be wholly (or for a high percentage)[3] produced in a single country of origin. A "cut and sew" model would allow products assembled in a member country to be eligible for preferential trade.

While restrictive, ROOs tend to increase the cost of trading by creating barriers between members and non-members, by increasing transaction costs for firms that deal with more than one FTA, and limiting access to cheaper imports from non-member countries. A restrictive "yarn forward" model defines a close model of integration and increases the distortive nature of the deal in terms of trade divergence, while a "cut and sew" model limits the trade distortions generated by a FTA (Augier et al. 2005).

While the details of this chapter of the agreement are not public, scholarly estimation tends to assume that the RCEP will employ a liberal

[2]ROOs are the criteria needed to determine the national source of a product: namely, where a product "actually" comes from. They are relevant because they duties and tariffs are applied according the country of origin. Methods and rules applied to establish the origin of a product vary greatly. If a product consists of components that are from more than one country, the criterion of substantial transformation is used to confer origin. Accordingly, the origin of the product is determined to be the last place in which it was "substantially transformed". However, determining what constitutes a substantial change can be quite complex. On the role of ROOs in multilateral trade agreements, see Estevadeordal et al. (2009).

[3]This percentage is calculated with different methods that are also under negotiations. Here we don't deal with the different methods. Details about these methods are beyond the scope of this chapter.

model, close to the "cut and sew" type. This is likely for several reasons. Firstly, because the RCEP, to deliver in terms of trade liberalization, needs the ROOs to be harmonized. In order to find a common ground, negotiators are likely to converge towards a "cut and sew" model, which is less costly in terms of trade divergence (Medalla 2015; Crook and Gordon 2017). Moreover, this model serves the interests of countries such as China, but also several ASEAN members, which are highly integrated into global and regional supply chains.

IP is another important pillar of any trade agreement of the new generation, since it deals with the complex relationship between protection of trademarks, incentives to innovation, and the possibility of making services, digital products, books and, importantly, medicines, accessible to low-income consumers (Medicins Sans Frontiers 2016; Townsend et al. 2016).[4] Information in this chapter of the agreement derives mainly from a document leaked in 2015, which includes the negotiating positions of several countries (Knowledge Ecology International 2015a). The leaked agreement helps our understanding of the nature of the negotiations between RCEP members.

As in other sectors, here the RCEP aims to be WTO consistent. In the realm of IP, therefore, the starting point was the adoption of the TRIPS agreement promoted by the WTO. Overall, the most advanced economies such as Japan, South Korea and Australia have pushed for a strict application of those norms in order to improve protection and market access. On the other hand, ASEAN countries have emphasized the necessity to find a compromise, especially in the pharmaceutical sector, where the trade-off between protection and cost for consumers is more acute (Yu 2017). China, together with India, which is by far the greatest producer of generic pharmaceutical products in Asia, appears to be taking a middle ground, promoting a position that aims to find a compromise between the two sides. China's position on IP in this case appears particularly interesting. In the years before and immediately after the accession to the WTO, Beijing employed a strategy of "selective adaptation" to TRIPS and IP property norms (Potter 2007). More recently, and particularly since the 2012 CPC congress, China has started

[4]For this reason, advocacy groups such Medicins Sans Frontiers have warned against the way in which IP is protected in the RCEP.

to emphasize the need of promoting "development by innovation". Therefore, it has shifted to a stricter position on IP (Stoianoff 2012). As Yu has stated: "In the end, this chapter will contain terms that offer more limited protection than the TPP IP chapter, but still more expansive protection than the TRIPS Agreement, or what is currently available in many Asian countries." (Yu 2017, p. 729). Ultimately, from this chapter emerges the research of a comprehensive and economically effective agreement that is balanced by the political will to preserve inclusiveness and respect for the widely different economic needs of a very diverse membership.

Another important aspect of the RCEP agreement concerns dispute settlement mechanisms. The nature of dispute settlement mechanisms is a very relevant feature of any contemporary FTA , since it establishes the possibility of neutral procedures aimed at enforcing the rule of law and the respect of the agreement between the parties.[5] From our theoretical standpoint, it is also relevant to highlight that this type of mechanisms should be associated with the solidarist order, since they tend to limit a states' sovereignty and self-determination, creating intrusive forms of governance that enable individuals and firms to protect their rights *vis-à-vis* other states.

Once again, the TPP can be considered a benchmark in this case. The TPP in fact promoted two very advanced dispute settlement mechanisms: one for disputes between states and the other, the Investor-State dispute settlement (ISDS) mechanism, aimed at regulating the disputes between firms and states (US Trade Representative 2016b; Chaisse 2012). Both were considered the most advanced type in specialized literature. These institutional mechanisms represent an example of the "economic solidarism" embedded in the agreement.

At the time of writing, it is not clear which type of mechanism the RCEP will adopt. In the leaked draft of the investment chapter, it appears that negotiators were considering the establishment of a ISDS mechanism allowing investors to sue states recipient of their investments (Knowledge Ecology International 2015a). Moreover, legal scholarship on the issue highlights that ASEAN+1 FTAs, as well as ASEAN itself,

[5] A dispute settlement mechanism refers to the presence of an independent organ of an international institution that has the right and the duty to settle disputes when a member considers the behaviour of another member contrary to the rules of the organization or the agreement in question. The main example of functioning dispute settlement mechanism is the Dispute Settlement Body of the World Trade Organization.

have a dispute settlement mechanism, inspired by the WTO dispute settlement mechanism (Gao and Liyu 2010).

Nevertheless, other analyses have doubted the effectiveness of the dispute settlement agreements in the ASEAN+1 agreements and highlighted that the RCEP is likely to follow a similar approach. Firstly, ASEAN+1 agreements foresee the necessity to establish ad hoc tribunals for state-to-state disputes. While the findings are binding, ASEAN states and their partners have never employed these procedures to resolve disputes, trying to reach diplomatic solutions before resorting to the formal dispute resolution process (Magiera 2017; Wang 2017). Moreover, other legal scholars underline how Beijing might favour an approach like that employed in the China–ASEAN FTA. That agreement favoured an approach aimed at reducing the capacity of the dispute settlement mechanism to overrule national regulation, and safeguarding the regulatory autonomy of those that receive investments.

On the issue of dispute settlement and protection of investments, China's interests are somewhat mixed. On the one hand, China has become an exporter of investments and, as a result, may be interested in establishing an effective ISDS mechanism. On the other hand, this would represent a significant deviation from its general preference towards non-interference, sovereignty and other pluralist features of the regional order.

From our standpoint, the research of a compromise between the protection of regulatory autonomy and the necessity of putting in place neutral and intrusive dispute mechanisms appears to be consistent with the Chinese approach to global governance. Such an approach highlights how Beijing is looking for a conciliation between the interest in establishing an effective trade agreement, capable of ensuring the protection of its outbound investments, and the normative orientation in favour of limits to intrusive institutional regulations, aimed at limiting political and economic sovereignty.

In order to understand the nature of the RCEP agreement, and the ideas and policy preferences, it will reflect, it is also important to underline which topics will be ignored or receive very limited coverage. The most relevant chapters are those dedicated to environment and labour standards. In these sectors, RCEP members considered the establishment of minimum standards in terms of labour protection and environment regulation as excessively intrusive forms of regulation, especially for developing countries. In this case, the pluralist and sovereigntist character of the RCEP is in stark contrast with the "economic solidarism" promoted by the TPP, which included both protection of worker rights, such as no use of child labour, minimum wages, and protection of environment, with particular refence to air and water pollution, as well as limits to exploitation of common resources such as fish and wildlife.

A final key difference with the TPP concerns measures of compensation. During the negotiations, it has emerged that low-income ASEAN countries as Cambodia, Myanmar or Laos are likely to suffer more from the abolition of tariffs. For this reason, RCEP negotiators are considering several different compensatory measures aimed at alleviating short-term losses, while facilitating the economic integration of less advanced economies. Principle 4 of the Guiding Principles explicitly states: "taking into consideration the different levels of development of the participating countries, the RCEP will include appropriate forms of flexibility including provision for special and differential treatment, plus additional flexibility to the least-developed ASEAN Member States." (Australian Department of Foreign Affairs and Trade 2012).

The idea of considering different stages of development, and adopting measures of compensation, contributes to political acceptability of the agreement itself. Ultimately, this feeds into the political narrative promoted by China, which challenged the will to impose a very costly "gold standard" promoted by the TPP members, with an approach that emphasized inclusion and harmony.

SOEs, Market and State Capitalism

The RCEP, as with the other two pillars of the Chinese regional project, involves a process of contestation and renegotiation of the market as a primary institution of the regional order. This does not mean that Beijing explicitly aims to export its economic model. Rather, it means that one of the main objectives of the RCEP is fostering a normative environment in which China's state capitalist practices can survive and prosper. This is consistent with the principle that RCEP should embrace diversity and promote economic integration with respect of each country's unique receipt to development and, above all, with China' s economic interests.

Today, China ranks second in the world for foreign direct investment (FDI) outflows (UNCTAD 2015). Most Chinese foreign direct investments are channelled through state-owned companies, with only three of the main 50 largest non-financial overseas investors not being controlled by SASAC (Liao and Zhang 2013).[6] Moreover, it has been calculated that up to 95% of the outward foreign investment lending provided by Chinese state-owned policy banks have been allocated to SOEs (Gallagher and Irwin 2014). In 2017, SOEs' outbound investments have been regulated by the SASAC, which has established that FDI should be required to follow different criteria, such as: being strategic and boosting capacity for innovation, leadership and the international competitiveness of the relevant SOE's business; being an appropriate investment, considering the size of the investment, as well as the financial position, industry and management experience and ability to adapt to risk of the investor; and offering a reasonable return (Damian and Ip 2017). While this new rules are likely to determine a reduction in the overall outflow of FDI, they are also aimed at consolidating the role of SOEs as exporters of capitals, limiting short-term speculative investments, favouring long-term projects oriented to innovation, access to technology and raw materials, and profitability. The fact that Chinese SOEs are the most important source of outbound FDI created the need to promote a regulatory environment that would not constrain their activities.

In order to understand the centrality of the issue of SOEs for the future of the regional economic order, it will be useful to compare the approach to this issue in the RCEP with the rules adopted by the TTP on those issues. One of the key purposes of the TPP was to promote the key principles of free market capitalism, advancing an economic environment hostile to state capitalism and to SOEs (Dian 2017). The chapter on SOEs embraced the principle of competitive neutrality, namely the principle according to which an economic entity should not have any competitive or regulatory advantage because of its ownership (Capobianco and Christiansen 2011; US Trade Representative 2016a). The chapter on SOE reflected the purpose of limiting the influence of the Chinese state-led sector in Asia, and ultimately aimed at limiting Beijing's capacity to use its companies to fulfil political needs, such as

[6] SASAC, the State-owned Asset Supervision and Administration Commission of the State Council, is the special commission that controls national level SOEs.

the acquisition of foreign technology, or using investment as a political reward. A similar treatment was dedicated to state-owned banks in the chapter dedicated to investments. The version of the TPP approved in 2016 could severely limit the possibility to invest in TPP member states for Chinese SOEs and Chinese state-controlled banks (Kawase 2014; Solis 2016).

This reflected both political and normative concerns. Normatively, the TPP aimed at promoting a "solidarist economic order" in which economic agents could freely operate through states' borders, transcending the limits imposed by their sovereignty and interventionism. For this reason, the TPP strictly limited the possibility of a state to intervene, distorting the market, both imposing the principles such as competitive neutrality, and allowing firms to directly sue the state in case of violations of international agreements with such mechanisms as the Investment Settlement Dispute Mechanism (ISDM). Politically, the US, under the Obama administration, considered the TPP an instrument to limit the penetration of the Chinese SOEs into the domestic markets of allies and their partners. A significant presence of the Chinese SOE was considered a risky development in the long term, since it could enhance Beijing's leverage on recipient states.

The principles and the interests China aims in promoting through the RCEP stand in opposition with the "solidarist" and free market principles of the TPP. Beijing's embracing of free trade and capitalism have a limit in the pluralist vision of the order it promotes, and on its preferences regarding sovereignty and state capitalism. Moreover, China needs to preserve the strategic role of its state-owned companies. As a result, the RCEP will not set clear limits to the legislative treatment of SOEs and state-owned banks, since it needs to promote a regulatory environment hospitable to Chinese outward investments that are largely led by SOEs and financed by state-owned banks. Details of competition policy, treatment of SOEs and public banks are not available at this stage.

The Guiding Principles foresee the possibility of a very loose regulation in the competition chapter, one that might more closely affect public companies, in the absence of a specific chapter dedicated to SOEs. According to the document:

> Provisions on competition will form the basis for parties to cooperate in the promotion of competition, economic efficiency, consumer welfare

> and the curtailment of anti-competitive practices while cognizant of the significant differences in the capacity and national regimes of RCEP participating countries in the area of competition. (Japanese Ministry of Economy, Trade and Industry 2012)

The respect for differences and national regimes opens the door to a chapter that would not limit the role of Chinese state-owned companies, which enjoy special legislative, fiscal and financial treatment, to investing and operating in other RCEP member states (Pearson 2015).

It is likely that these issues will be regulated following the same approach adopted by China in other bilateral and multilateral FTAs. Among all the FTAs signed by China, only two have detailed chapters on competition policy and SOEs: the bilateral agreement with Switzerland and Iceland. These agreements include references to the principle of competitive neutrality, and put in place joint advisory committees for dispute resolution (Chen and Whalley 2014). In practice, however, they hardly put in place any limit to the special treatment of SOEs. More specifically, these agreements include the necessity of openness and cooperation, but do not include any binding rule on information and transparency. Moreover, the agreements underline that they don't limit national sovereignty and independence in the national competition policies.

Conclusion

At the time of writing, member states are still negotiating the RCEP agreement. Mega trade agreements always entail lengthy and complex negotiations and are likely to be finalized after significant delays. Moreover, as testified by the case of the TPP, even after the final agreement is reached, it is possible that one or more states could decide to refuse to ratify it, jeopardizing many years of negotiations. From this point of view, the RCEP could encounter new and unforeseen political obstacles, especially if relations between China and India continue along the recent downward path (Jaishankar 2017).

Nevertheless, with TPP and TTIP stopped by the Trump administration, the RCEP remains the most significant, multilateral trade initiative under negotiation. This is in itself a very important development from the perspective of the evolution of the regional and global economic order. China is currently the major power that is investing more, politically and economically, in initiatives aimed at promoting commercial integration and economic connectivity.

The window of opportunity opened by the retreat of the US has given Beijing a very significant opportunity to shape the regional economic order according to its preferences. Firstly, China prefers an order that has a markedly "Asian" shape, centred on its leadership and its centrality. This entails the marginalization of the US from the process of regional commercial integration. Moreover, the RCEP foresees the participation of India and Japan, two countries that did not welcome other Chinese initiatives. Up to the beginning of 2017, Japan refused to participate in BRI and AIIB, considering them a potential threat to its economic interests, and to its preferred model of an open "trans-Pacific" template of regional integration, rooted in the leadership of the US (Fujiwara 2016). The Indian position on the other Chinese initiatives is more mixed. India is a founding member of AIIB, but has demonstrated itself more sceptical on B&R projects. According to Li Hao, as far as its position in the RCEP is concerned, it seems that two major critical projects are at stake: the bilateral relations and cooperation respectively with China and Japan, and the huge trade deficit among member-states; part of the agreement. As with China, it is precisely the vast amount in terms of trade deficit India has with Beijing that also counts as the greatest challenge to the deepening of Sino-India relations. Although India's participation in the RCEP negotiations significantly promotes foreign trade, it does not necessarily imply the rapid growth of Indian exports resulting with total trade liberalization (Li 2014).

Despite these concerns, both Japan and India are fully participating in the negotiations for the RCEP, implicitly recognizing that, after the stall of the TPP, the agreement now represents the most significant opportunity for promoting regional economic integration in Asia.

As we described above, China's approach rejects the idea of the "gold standard" pursued by the TPP and its members to promote a more gradualist and inclusive approach. The Chinese approach has often been dismissed as "low quality" in the specialized literature, especially in the field of international economics and international political economy. Here, we neither wish to dispute this point nor disagree with the fact that a TPP-like approach can be considered more efficient in terms of pure economic gains. Here, we wish to stress the appeal of the approach promoted through the RCEP, especially when compared to the "gold standard approach" employed by the TPP. The RCEP is far less costly for its members than TPP, in both political and economic terms. It is less intrusive, since it does not require deep structural reforms. The RCEP will not force its members to introduce minimum standards in areas such as labour and environment, or to downsize and privatize SOEs and state-owned banks. As a result, it will have a more limited impact on the socio-economic structures of member states, and will also be easier for governments and key political and economic constituencies to accept. Equally importantly, the ideas underpinning the RCEP and, more broadly, China's approach to trade agreements, positively resonate in many Asian countries. Concepts of gradualism, respect of local conditions of development, limited interference, and respect of other states' national sovereignty make the agreement much more acceptable, compared to an extremely intrusive agreement, such as TPP.

Finally, the way in which China has approached trade negotiations represent a further example of how the Chinese leadership is increasingly capable of fitting its policy initiative within a master narrative, composed of post-colonial and neo-Confucian elements. On the one hand, China's economic role is presented as that of a natural leader, able to provide order, prosperity and harmony. On the other hand, Beijing present itself as the state that can drive the renascence of the post-colonial world, and its principles and its needs, while resisting the extremely intrusive forms of economic governance promoted by the West and the US.

The likely political consequences of the RCEP have been neglected by scholars and analysts, since most analyses have looked primarily at gains in terms of GDP, possible increases in trade volume, and trade diversion. The RCEP, once approved, might deliver other equally important benefits for China. It could contribute to the acceptability of a future leadership role, at least in the economic realm, and consolidate key aspects of a regional economic order consistent with Beijing's preferences.

Bibliography

Ahn, Dukgeun. 2013. "Dispute Settlement Systems in Asian FTAs: Issues and Problems." *Asian Journal of WTO and International Health Policy* 8 (2): 421–443.

ASEAN. 2016. "Framework for Regional Comprehensive Economic Partnership." Available at http://asean.org/?static_post=asean-framework-for-regional-comprehensive-economic-partnership. Accessed 27 May 2016.

Augier, Patricia, Michael Gasiorek, and Charles Lai Tong. 2005. "The Impact of Rules of Origin on Trade Flows." *Economic Policy* 20 (43): 568–624.

Australian Department of Foreign Affairs and Trade. 2012, August 30. *Guiding Principles and Objectives for Negotiating the Regional Comprehensive Economic Partnership.* Canberra. http://dfat.gov.au/trade/agreements/rcep/Documents/guiding-principles-rcep.pdf.

Bell, Daniel A. 2016. *The China Model: Political Meritocracy and the Limits of Democracy.* Princeton, NJ: Princeton University Press.

Bhagwati, Jagdish N. 2008. *Termites in the Trading System: How Preferential Agreements Undermine Free Trade.* Oxford: Oxford University Press.

Capobianco, Antonio, and Hans Christiansen. 2011. *Competitive Neutrality and State-Owned Enterprises: Challenges and Policy Options.* Paris: OECD Corporate Governance Working Papers 1. Retrieved from http://www.oecd-ilibrary.org/governance/competitive-neutrality-and-state-owned-enterprises_5kg9xfgjdhg6-en.

Chaisse, Julienne. 2012. "TPP Agreement. Innovation in Investment Rule Making." In *The Trans-Pacific Partnership: A Quest for a Twenty-First Century Trade Agreement*, edited by Chin Leng Lim, Deborah K. Elms, and Patrick Low, 147–156. Cambridge: Cambridge University Press.

Chen, Hejing, and John Whalley. 2014. *The State-Owned Enterprises Issue in China's Prospective Trade Negotiations.* CIGI papers 48.

Chinese Ministry of Commerce. 2017, March 1. "谈判 或进入加速期" [RCEP: Accelerating the Negotiations]. Available at http://fta.mofcom.gov.cn/article/rcep/rcepgfgd/201703/34298_1.html. Accessed 25 September 2017.

Crook, Wayne, and Jenny Gordon. 2017, May 2014. "Rules of Origin: Can the Noodle Bowl of Trade Agreements Be Untangled?" *Australian Productivity Commission Staff Research Note.* Canberra. Available at https://www.pc.gov.au/research/supporting/rules-of-origin/rules-of-origin.pdf. Accessed 23 October 2017.

Dai, Xinyuan. 2015. "Who Defines the Rules of the Game in East Asia? The Trans-Pacific Partnership and the Strategic Use of International Institutions." *International Relations of the Asia-Pacific* 15 (1): 1–25.

Damian, Tony, and Karen Ip. 2017, February 27. *Will the Rooster Crow? Chinese Outbound Investment in 2017.* Herbert Free Hills, Legal Briefing.

Dent, Christopher M. 2013. "Paths Ahead for East Asia and Asia–Pacific Regionalism." *International Affairs* 89 (4): 963–985.

Dian, Matteo. 2017. "The Strategic Value of the Trans-Pacific Partnership and the Consequences of Abandoning for the US Role in Asia." *International Politics* 54 (5): 583–587.

Elms, Deborah. 2013. "The Trans-Pacific Partnership: The Challenges of Unraveling the Noodle Bowl." *International Negotiation* 18 (1): 25–47.

Emmers, Ralf, and John Ravenhill. 2011. "The Asian and Global Financial Crises: Consequences for East Asian Regionalism." *Contemporary Politics* 17 (2): 133–149.

Estevadeordal, Antoni, Jeremy Harris, and Kati Suominen. 2009. "Harmonizing Preferential Rules of Origin Regimes around the World." In *Multilateralizing Regionalism: Challenges for the Global Trade System*, edited by Richard Baldwin and Patrick Low, 427–549. Cambridge: Cambridge University Press.

Ford, Christopher A. 2015. "The Party and the Sage: Communist China's Use of Quasi-Confucian Rationalizations for One-Party Dictatorship and Imperial Ambition." *Journal of Contemporary China* 24 (96): 1032–1047.

Freddie, Kleiner. 2017, March 6. "美国推出TPP 将 让中国主导亚太贸易?" [US Exit from TPP Will Allow China to Dominate Asia-Pacific Trade?]. *Financial Times Chinese*. Available at http://www.ftchinese.com/story/001071633#adchannelID=2000. Accessed 2 October 2017.

Fujiwara, Hidehito. 2016, August. "One Belt, One Road, A Japanese Perspective." *International Institute for Asian Studies*, Newsletter 74. http://iias.asia/the-newsletter/article/one-belt-one-road-japanese-perspective.

Fukunaga, Yoshifumi, and Ikumo Isono. 2013. "Taking ASEAN+1 FTAs Towards the RCEP: A Mapping Study." *ERIA Discussion Paper Series* 2: 1–37.

Gallagher, Kevin P., and Amos Irwin. 2014. "Exporting National Champions: China's Outward Foreign Direct Investment Finance in Comparative Perspective." *China & World Economy* 22 (6): 1–21.

Gao, Henry, and Han Liyu. 2010. "China's Experience in Utilising the WTO Dispute Settlement Mechanism." In *Dispute Settlement at The WTO: The Developing Country Experience*, edited by Gregory Shaffer and Ricardo Meléndez-Ortiz, 137–173. Cambridge: Cambridge University Press.

Jaishankar, Dhruva. 2017, August 10. "Why Are China and India in a Border Standoff?" Brooking Institution. Available at https://www.brookings.edu/opinions/why-are-china-and-india-in-a-border-standoff/. Accessed 1 September 2017.

Japanese Ministry of Economy, Trade and Industry. 2012. *Guiding Principles and Objectives for Negotiating the Regional Comprehensive Economic Partnership*. Available at http://www.meti.go.jp/policy/trade_policy/east_asia/dl/RCEP_GP_EN.pdf. Accessed 27 October 2017.

Kawase, Tsuyoshi. 2014. *Trans Pacific Partnership and Rule Making to Regulate the State-Owned Enterprises*. Tokyo: RIETI Policy Update 53.

Knowledge Ecology International. 2015a, October 15. *RCEP IP Chapter*. Washington, DC, and Geneva: Knowledge Ecology International. Available at http://keionline.org/node/2472. Accessed 12 September 2017.

Knowledge Ecology International. 2015b, October 16. *RCEP Investment Chapter*. Washington, DC, and Geneva: Knowledge Ecology International. Available at https://www.keionline.org/node/2474. Accessed 12 September 2017.

Li, Hao. 2014. "印度参与区域全面经济伙伴关系谈判的动因及制约因素探析" [Motivations and Constraints of India's Engagement in Regional Comprehensive Economic Partnership Negotiations]. 亚太经济 [*Asia-Pacific Economy*] 5: 75–78.

Liao, Shuping, and Yongsheng Zhang. 2013. *A New Context for Managing Overseas Direct Investment by Chinese State-Owned Enterprises*. EABER Working Paper 83.

Magiera, Stephen L. 2017. *International Investment Agreements and Investor-State Disputes: A Review and Evaluation for Indonesia*. Economic Research Institute for AEAN and East Asia. Jakarta: ERIA Discussion Paper Series.

Medalla, Erlinda M. 2015. *Toward an Enabling Set of Rules of Origin for the Regional Comprehensive Economic Partnertship*. PIDS Discussion Paper Series 29.

Medicins Sans Frontiers. 2016, November. *Intellectual Property Chapter and the Impact on Access to Medicines*. Available at https://www.msfaccess.org/sites/default/files/IP_RCEP_%20IPChapteranalysis_MSF_Access%20to%20Medicines_2016_ENG.pdf. Accessed 20 September 2017.

Ministry of Commerce, People's Republic of China. 2014, September 1. "Give Play of China's Important Role and Accelerate RCEP's Negotiations." Available at http://fta.mofcom.gov.cn/enarticle/rcepen/enrcepnews/201411/18815_1.html. Accessed 23 April 2017.

Panda, Jagannath P. 2014. "Factoring the RCEP and the TPP: China, India and the Politics of Regional Integration." *Strategic Analysis* 38 (1): 49–67.

Pearson, Magaret M. 2015. "State Owned Business and Party—State Regulation in China's Modern Political Economy." In *State Capitalism, Institutional Adaptation, and the Chinese Miracle*, edited by Barry Naughton and Kellee S. Tsai, 27–45. Cambridge: Cambridge University Press.

Potter, Pitman B. 2007. "China and the International Legal System: Challenges of Participation." In *China's Legal System: New Developments, New Challenges*, edited by Donald C. Clark, 145–164. Cambridge: Cambridge University Press.

Solis, Mireya. 2016. *The Trans-Pacific Partnership: The Politics of Openness and Leadership in the Asia-Pacific*. Asia Working Paper Group 6. Brookings Institution.

Stoianoff, Natalie. 2012. "The Influence of the WTO over China's Intellectual Property Regime." *Sydney Law Review* 34 (1): 65–89.

Townsend, Belinda, Deborah Gleeson, and Ruth Lopert. 2016. "The Regional Comprehensive Economic Partnership, Intellectual Property Protection, and Access to Medicines." *Asia Pacific Journal of Public Health* 28 (8): 682–693.

United Nations Conference on Trade and Development. 2015. "World Investment Report 2015." New York.

US Trade Representative. 2016a. *Trans Pacific Partnership Final Full Text: Chapter 17, State-Owned Enterprises and Designated Monopolies*. Available at https://ustr.gov/sites/default/files/TPP-Final-Text-State-Owned-Enterprises-and-Designated-Monopolies.pdf.

US Trade Representative. 2016b. *Trans Pacific Partnership Final Full Text Final Full Text: Chapter 28, Dispute Settlement.* Available at https://ustr.gov/sites/default/files/TPP-Chapter-Summary-Dispute-Settlement.pdf. Accessed 11 September 2017.

Wang, Heng. 2017. "The RCEP and Its Investment Rules: Learning from Past Chinese FTAs." *The Chinese Journal of Global Governance* 3 (2): 1–27.

Wilson, Jeffrey D. 2015. "Mega-Regional Trade Deals in the Asia-Pacific: Choosing between the TPP and RCEP?" *Journal of Contemporary Asia* 45 (2): 345–353.

World Economic Forum. 2017, January 18. *Xi Jinping Full Speech.* https://www.weforum.org/agenda/2017/01/full-text-of-xi-jinping-keynote-at-the-world-economic-forum.

Yu, Peter K. 2017. "The RCEP and Trans-Pacific Intellectual Property Norms." *Vanderbilt Journal of Transnational Law* 50 (3): 673–740.

Zhang, Jianping. 2014. "中国推进区域全面经济伙伴关系的战略考量" [Strategic Thinking on Promoting Regional Comprehensive Economic Partnership for China]. *Asia-Pacific Economy* 2: 34–139.

Zou, Guoyong, and Linling Wu. 2016. "TPP, RCEP, 背景下的中国东盟自冒区建设挑战与应对" [The Construction of China-ASEAN FTA under TPP and RCEP: Challenges and Responses]. *Journal of Jishou University* 37 (2): 53–61.

CHAPTER 6

Conclusion

Abstract This book has described the role of China's regional initiatives in the process of contestation of key pillars of the regional order in Asia. Contrarily of realist predictions China is not behaving as a revisionist state, destined to subvert the current international order. Beijing is rather promoting a selective contestation of the current regional order, advancing its preferences, its interests and its values. China has developed a narrative based on post-colonial and neo-Confucian elements that has gained a certain traction in the Asia. Ultimately, through Belt and Road Initiative (BRI), Asia Infrastructure and Investment Bank (AIIB) and Regional Comprehensive Economic Partnership (RCEP) has been proposing itself as potential regional leader in the wide Eurasian context. Finally, China's initiatives appear to be destined to strengthen the pluralist features of the regional order in Asia.

Keywords International order · New type of great power relations China Dream · Regionalism · English School

This research has analysed the three main initiatives that have characterized China's blueprint for regional economic governance under the leadership of Xi Jinping, the Belt and Road Initiative (BRI), the Asia Infrastructure and Investment Bank (AIIB) and the Regional Comprehensive Economic Partnership (RCEP). We looked both at the ideational and normative foundations of those initiatives, and at their political purposes. Moreover, we put forward several hypotheses on how these initiatives might affect

M. Dian and S. Menegazzi, *New Regional Initiatives in China's Foreign Policy*, https://doi.org/10.1007/978-3-319-75505-2_6

China's role in Asia and beyond. Our analysis led to several significant conclusions. From the vantage point of our analysis, China does not appear to be the revisionist state described by realist analyses and by supporters of the "Thucydides Trap" metaphor (Allison 2017).

Under Xi Jinping, Beijing has now definitively abandoned the low-key posture inspired by Deng's motto, "hide your strength and bide your time", (韬光养晦 *taoguang yanghui*) in order to embrace a new proactive foreign policy rooted in the concept of "striving for achievement" (奋发有位 *fenfa youwei*) (Callahan 2016; Yan 2014). However, this does not mean that China has turned itself into an overtly revisionist state, as predicted by structural realists. China in fact is not working to overtly overthrow or disrupt the global order. The Chinese leadership is aware that the Chinese rise has been possible by virtue of the current international order. In John Ikenberry's words, the liberal US-based order is "easier to join that to overthrow" (Ikenberry 2011). China's success has, in fact, been due to the openness of the US-led order and a certain degree of flexibility among its main institutions, that accommodated the economic and political ascendency of a returning great power such as China. China's economic structure, characterized by an investment-led, export-oriented model, creates the need to work within an open international order. China's very cultivated self-image reflects this need. This clearly emerges, when considering recent Chinese positions on economic globalization. During the famous Davos speech, Xi Jinping presented China as the last bastion of economic globalization and free trade, at a time when the winds of populism and protectionism agitated the West.

However, simply describing contemporary China as an "order taker" would definitively miss several key aspects of the Chinese relationship with the current regional and global order, ignoring the most consequential aspects of strategy promoted by Xi and the Fifth Generation of Leaders. The current Chinese strategy can be best characterized by a selective contestation of the regional and global order. In terms of order, China means to contest, reshape and reform the international order, according to its interests as well as its ideas and values. Xi's blueprint is focused mostly on the regional level. However, this process will also have crucial consequences at the global level.

Our theoretical approach, inspired by the English School of IR, allows us to effectively describe this process, concentrating on key primary institutions of the international order. Focusing on primary institutions in the English School sense, we have observed how the creation of new

China-led institutions involves a process of contestation and renegotiation of key normative pillars of the regional order. Here, we have focused on four: great power management; geography; sovereignty; and market.

China's regionalist initiatives involve a significant process of renegotiation of great power management in Asia. This institution generally refers to the capacity of great powers to limit conflict and impose order. Classic interpretations of this approach refer mostly to the necessity to avoid war between great powers, finding a common ground in terms of recognition of mutual interests and some commonality in terms of legitimacy. Here, we refer more explicitly to the mutual recognition of the leadership of great powers, and their capacity to promote new forms of order, both in the realm of "high politics" and in the realm of economic cooperation. In line with more recent analyses of great power management, we stress both the vertical dimension (a great power recognized by smaller states) and the horizontal dimension (between great powers) of this institution.

From this perspective, what happens with China's regional initiatives is related to a process of recognition. China has gradually been recognized not just as a legitimate great power, but also as an order maker, capable of reshaping the geographical, normative, and institutional contours of the regional order.

It is worth noting that China itself did not want to assume this role until recently. Under Deng and Jiang, China explicitly avoided embracing any role in processes of regional governance. Under Hu Jintao, especially after its access to WTO, it assumed a more relevant role, but continued to avoid any leadership role, encouraging ASEAN to maintain its cherished "driving seat". Under Xi, with BRI, AIIB and RCEP, the PRC has, de facto, assumed a leading position, promoting new institutions, inspired by Chinese norms and values, legitimized by a distinctively Chinese narrative, and, as in the case of the AIIB or the BRI Forum, located in Beijing. Significantly, this has corresponded with a process of recognition of the Chinese role as order maker. Other states, great powers and smaller states, in Asia and beyond, have recognized and legitimized China's initiatives, acknowledging its newfound status. This is a relevant and very recent change. No observer of the Chinese and Asian affairs, two or even one decade ago, could reasonably have predicted that China would successfully promote three major initiatives in the realm of global governance. The rise of China, as well as the process of recognition of its role that has unfolded in recent years, has made these initiatives possible, but also successful, at least so far.

The level of the maturity and the speed of the process of recognition of China as an order maker has surprised most observers. When China promoted the AIIB at the beginning of 2014, hardly any policymakers or analysts, either in China or in the West, predicted the extent of its success. When it was launched, the AIIB was aimed mostly at Asian states, even if was formally open to extra-regional actors. The unexpected participation of the UK opened the door for the participation of several other European countries, such as Germany, France, and Italy as founding members.

Our analysis, however, testifies how this process is far from complete, particularly in the horizontal dimension, concerning relations between great powers in the region. If we look at AIIB, China's status of "institution building" has been recognized by Asian states aside from Japan. BRI has been welcomed by the vast majority of Asian states. However, it experienced significant resistance from India and Japan.[1] RCEP, which is less explicitly Sino-centric compared to the other BRI and AIIB, involves the participation of all the ASEAN+6 states, including Japan and India.

The process of renegotiation of great power management in Asia experienced significant resistance from the most relevant extra-reginal actor in Asia, the US. The American resistance appeared clear in the case of AIIB. The position of the Obama administration was formally based on uncertainty regarding the legal and economic standards that the new institution would have followed. Practically, however, Washington feared the expansion of the Chinese influence and failed to recognize China's role as legitimate order maker. As a result, it asked its allies and partners to abstain from adhering. This move turned out to be unsuccessful, since only Japan followed through, while a close partner of the UK lamented the American interference on the issue. This opened the door to the far less publicized but equally relevant participation of other key European states.

In the case of RCEP, the role of US resistance has evolved significantly with the election of Donald Trump. The Obama administration, under the rubric of the Pivot to Asia, promoted its vision of an integrated Trans-Pacific economic region, based on a solidarist understanding of the regional order, free market capitalism, and American leadership. The TTP embodied this effort of reasserting Washington's capacity to act as order maker, despite the expansion of China's economic clout. The Pivot to Asia ultimately aimed at curbing Beijing's capacity to shape the normative and institutional contours of the region.

[1] As we saw in Chapter 3, the Japanese position has evolved since the beginning of 2017.

Up to 2016, therefore, the RCEP was part of a contestation of templates in which two models of regionalism competed and partially overlapped: on the one hand, a model of Sino-centric regionalism based on state capitalism and other "pluralist" values, on the other, a US-led Trans-Pacific model, rooted in free market capitalism.

The election of Donald Trump, his protectionist "American first" manifesto, and the subsequent abandonment of the Pivot and the Trans Pacific Partnership (TPP), turned the realm of economic governance into an uncontested political space. This offered China the possibility to promote solutions inspired by Chinese interests and values. From this perspective, it clearly emerges how Trump has actively worked to "make China Great Again", opening a window of opportunity for political and institutional leadership in Asia.

China's regionalist project also involves a process of contestation of the geographical boundaries of the region. Before the Asian financial crisis of 1997–1998, China's involvement in regional governance was extremely limited, since Beijing feared that it might lead to limits to its sovereignty and self-determination. The Asian financial crisis led to a complete change in the Chinese approach to regional governance, for two main reasons. The first was the perception, shared by many Asian states, of the role Washington and the main international financial institutions had played in the crisis. Secondly, the Chinese government understood that a major engagement in the process of region-building was fundamental to securing its interests and to ensuring the stability of the economic order upon which the Chinese rise rested. Key initiatives in regional governance at this time focused on the ASEAN+3 framework. Examples are the Chiang Mai Initiative and the Asia Bond Market Initiative.

During the Hu era, the Chinese approach carefully balanced the objective of nurturing East Asian forms of regionalism aimed at limiting the US influence in the region, and policies aimed at balancing the Japanese influence, together with genuine interests around the necessity to foster financial stability in Asia (Chin and Stubbs 2011). Since the mid-2000s, China has appeared less concerned with the Japanese influence and progressively more inclined to consider the new regional fora as instruments aimed at limiting the American influence and creating a regional order open to a role of great power and as a provider of public goods for China.

During the Xi era, China has increasingly seen itself as the centre of a broadly defined Asian region, extending from the Central Asian steppe to the East and South-East China Sea. On the one hand, this is because East Asia is an extremely crowded and contested space, in economic, normative and strictly strategic terms. The enduring American presence, reaffirmed during the Pivot to Asia, and the resistance to a Chinese leadership role by South Korea and Japan, have led Beijing to look to other areas that could be more welcoming for Chinese initiatives. On the other hand, the ascent of a neo-Confucian narrative, based on the centrality of China as the natural leader of the entire Asian continent, has led to broadening the horizon on contemporary regional strategies and including a wider definition of the Chinese role.

This redefinition of the geographical boundaries is accompanied by the idea that the region should be exclusive: namely, protected by extra regional-influences, and in particular by the influence of the US. As Xi himself underlined in 2014:

> In the final analysis, it is for the people of Asia to run the affairs of Asia, solve the problems of Asia and uphold the security of Asia. The people of Asia have the capability and wisdom to achieve peace and stability in the region through enhanced cooperation. (Xi 2014)

The third fundamental primary institution affected by the Chinese regionalist project is sovereignty. China, since the beginning of the process of reform and opening, has embraced the Five Principles of Peaceful Co-Existence and a pluralist understanding of the international order. From a Chinese perspective, states should find their own path to development and modernity. The Chinese experience is considered as a useful example for developing countries. Nevertheless, China, does not aim to export it. Rather, it aims to develop mutually advantageous relations and win-win forms of cooperation, despite possible differences of values and political regimes. China's approach to BRI, AIIB and RCEP appears, therefore, in strong continuity with previous policies. These initiatives in fact reflect the will locating the norms of mutual respect of sovereignty, self-determination and non-interference at the centre of the Asian regional order.

This research has stressed how the attempt to consolidate and even deepen the pluralist and sovereigntist features of the regional order has found some significant limits, in particular when China has promoted deeper forms of economic connectivity. This appears quite clear in the case of BRI and RCEP and to some extent also in the AIIB's case.

As we saw in Chapter 3, the BRI entails a huge and very risky gamble. BRI is based on two assumptions: China will have stable and friendly relations with its BRI partners; and states that host long term infrastructural investments will be peaceful and politically stable. Both these assumptions involve a significant degree of optimism for two reasons. Many states that will host key infrastructural projects are not domestically unstable. There are cases of regime instability, such as Pakistan and Kazakhstan; case of ethnic and religious separatism in provinces that should host major infrastructures, such as Belochistan; and cases of areas subject to border disputes, such as Kashmir. In cases of political instability, regime change, or radical foreign policy—shifts affecting host countries—China will have very significant incentives to abandon the principle of non-interference and to embrace an interventionist policy. China's deployment of PLA navy vessels to guard the post of Gwadar, is the first evidence of this tendency.

Fear of an expansion of the Chinese presence in their traditional sphere of influence might lead to more resistance to Chinese initiatives. Ultimately, major Asian powers such as India and possibly Russia might work to undermine the Chinese project, in order to regain influence in certain regions in South and Central Asia. These developments could also create incentives to involve China in local disputes.

RCEP entails a different set of challenges for China's blueprint of a solidarist regional order. As we saw in Chapter 5, China, through RCEP, has proposed an alternative to free market-oriented and "solidarist"[2] forms of economic integration. Nevertheless, the technical task of promoting a free trade agreement of the new generation involves different compromises with the principles of respect of sovereignty and non-interference. An agreement that aims at overcoming non-tariff barriers needs to put forward several regulations that would breach national sovereignty. RCEP will not limit the sovereignty of states as much as TPP would have done, leaving sectors such as State Owned Enterprises (SOEs), competition, labour and environment poorly regulated, or not regulated at all. Nevertheless, RCEP is likely to propose some intrusive form of regulation, particularly in the realm of dispute settlement, investments, Intellectual property (IP), and rules of origin.

[2] Here we don't mean any form of solidarity between actors involved. In line with the English School meaning of the term, we mean forms of governance that regulate and protect the role of individuals, as economic actors, from the intervention of the state.

major political narratives driving Beijing's "core interests" in foreign policy, but particularly "South-South" relations with developing countries (Ferchen 2014). Through this narrative, China has been able to construct an image of a country ready not only to alter status quo dynamics at the international level, but also to safeguard the interests of developing countries (Ministry of Foreign Affairs, Federal Democratic Republic of Ethiopia 2014).[3] With Xi Jinping assuming office, the strategy has become somehow even more sophisticated, whereby the image of China as a developing country has grown in parallel with that of a country strongly benefiting economic globalization. Chinese leaders have stressed the positive consequences of increasing public diplomacy among China and its neighbours, i.e., through the promotion of the idea of building a community of common destiny. However, at the same time, they have been able to promote a series of economic initiatives that have to be intended also as part of a mercantilist effort to reinforce China's geostrategic interests and influence in the world (Ferchen 2017).

As Chapter 2 dealing with the Chinese narrative demonstrated, the post-colonial and neo-Confucian concepts have been useful to enhance the legitimacy of China's foreign policy as well as to a attract support from developing countries and emerging economies. Based on the post-colonial nationalism narrative, China distances itself from former (Western) colonial states pursuing power politics in the world's peripheral areas, while threatening their foreign policy principles such as sovereignty, non-interference and the right to self-determination. This is because Chinese leaders still regard national humiliation—indeed the so-called Century of National Humiliation—as the official narrative to tell China's story in the twenty-first century. To some extent, the same narrative, albeit to a different degree, is affecting China's normative considerations and behaviour within most of multilateral initiatives being promoted by Beijing in the global governance domain. For instance, in the AoA of the AIIB, "political sovereignty" represents an essential principle which member countries should withstand in order to be part of the bank. Even though it is unlikely that countries will be asked to back off for failure to comply with such recommendations, it is still a first attempt by the (China-led) bank to clarify the unwanted influence of political issues in the economic and financial circumstances of

[3] Ethiopia, for instance, looks positively at how China addressed major globalization challenges while guaranteeing the interests of developing countries.

the AIIB's financed projects. Likewise, the RCEP is expected to be different from other multilateral trade agreements. It is less ambitious in regulatory terms, meaning that thanks to softer standards that are apt to reflect the different levels of development of participating economies. Consequently, developing countries will feel less threatened, when asked to comply with "top-down" rules and practices.

Likewise, the neo-Confucian narrative has been the backbone to promoting China's globalization-friendly practice of win-win diplomacy, while also prioritizing China's economic development and foreign policy interests. More specifically, neo-Confucian ideas of pursuing merit and harmony at the international level have been presented by Chinese leaders as a normative alternative to Western ideas and the international order associated with them. For instance, Wang Yi, the Minister of Foreign Affairs, affirmed that international relations—from economics to politics, from cultural to security issues—should be of a new type of win-win cooperation:

> China works to promote win-win cooperation both through policy initiatives and with real actions. China calls for the building of a new type of international relations of win-win cooperation, a relationship that we believe are for the dignity, development interests and peace and security of all countries and peoples. China's diplomacy will be firmly rooted in the conditions both at home and in the wider world to serve the fundamental interests of the Chinese people and people of other countries. Let us be firm in our commitment to peaceful development and work together in win-win cooperation to usher in even brighter prospects for the benefit of all in the world. (Ministry of Foreign Affairs 2015)

To this extent, we believe that China has been able to elaborate an alternative project for regional and global economic governance, based on principles, norms and values that are alternative to those of the West. This book has shown that this alternative can be appealing to developing countries, not simply for economic reasons.

In the African continent or Latin America, many states suffered the intrusion of Western great powers in the colonial era and during the Cold War. The same holds true in the Asian context during the 1997 financial crisis. For instance, today is widely believed that the financial chaos of major East Asian economies in mid-1997, i.e. the IMF imposing excessive conditionality on the East Asian economies, made the economic and financial consequences of the financial crisis that hit, Indonesia, Thailand and Korea, Malaysia and the Philippines much deeper and long lasting (Radelet and Sachs 1998). Through the new initiatives exemplified within the previous chapters, i.e., the AIIB, the RCEP and to a lesser extent the BRI, the Chinese narrative and the emphasis on the post colonial overtones as well as the special needs of developing countries entails the fact that no conditionality of any type should be applied through the involvement of multilateral development banks or, more generally, through infrastructural development projects. In practice, however, it remains to be seen to what extent this will be a feasible option. As we saw in Chapter 3, the majority of the AIIB's projects are co-financed with Western financial institutions, some of which utilize the same conditionality that China believes should be avoided. The same holds true for the BRI. When it comes to its foreign policy and core interests, China is keen to defend sovereignty and the non-interference principles. However, as shown in Chapter 4, this may not hold true with China "interfering", through infrastructural projects, in third countries economic and political activities.

When looking at Chinese political narratives, one last reflection concerns the ascent malaise of Western-style democracy in the world, today supported by growing waves of inequality, populism and a scarce growth rate within and among major developed economies. China, under Xi's leadership has promoted a comprehensive blueprint for economic governance in Asia and beyond. The possible success of this project is deeply intertwined with the future of the economic and political order in Asia and globally for a number of reasons. Firstly, China's proposals are inherently pluralist in nature, being rooted on concepts such as sovereignty and non-interference, together with a strong guidance of the state in the economic realms. In this sense, their success would reverse a tendency that have characterized global governance since the end of the Cold War, namely the attempts to promote a solidarist political order, in which rights of states are eroded *vis-à-vis* the rights of individuals (and firms). China's possible success would ultimately represent an important step toward the return of more explicitly state centric forms of regional and global order. A final point regards the relationship between the competition between pluralist and solidarist forms of economic governance. The United States and the West, since the Cold War have been promoting forms of economic governance that have deprived the state of many instruments of control over global economic flows.

Economic liberalization and globalization have contributed to the rise of inequality in Western democracy. This in turn has fuelled the rise of populism and the current democratic malaise. The election of Donald Trump in the US and Brexit are just the two most significant effect of this phenomenon.

In this context, the Chinese proposals are even more significant. China has been challenging the main assumptions on which the Western approach to global economic governance was founded upon. Firstly, China has been making the case that liberal democracy is not an essential element for modernization. On the contrary Beijing has found its own receipt for modernity and economic development. China's regional initiatives amplified this message: Asian countries and other developing countries can reject both Western democracy and Western influence and achieve modernity and development, with the Chinese help. Secondly, China's criticism goes even further. The malaise of the West represents a threat to economic globalization. The rise of populism and protectionism are depicted as symptoms of the weakness of the democratic system, compared to the Chinese alternative, inspired to the Confucian concept of leadership by virtue, knowledge and experience.

While many commentators would be ready to dismiss this message as pure propaganda it is important to understand the influence and the appeal these ideas have in developing countries through Asia and beyond.

Bibliography

Allison, Graham T. 2017. *Destined for War: Can America and China Escape Thucydides's Trap?* Boston, MA: Houghton Mifflin Harcourt.

Callahan, William A. 2016. "China's "Asia Dream": The Belt Road Initiative and the New Regional Order." *Asian Journal of Comparative Politics* 1 (3): 226–243.

Chin, Gregory, and Richard Stubbs. 2011. "China Regional Institution-Building and the China–ASEAN Free Trade Area." *Review of International Political Economy* 183 (2): 277–298.

Ferchen, Matt. 2014. "The Contradictions of China's Developing Country's Identity." Caijing.com.cn [陈茂修的个人空间]. http://blog.caijing.com.cn/expert_article-151713-70596.shtml.

Ferchen, Matt. 2017. "How China Is Using Its Economic Goals to Assert Global Influence." Beijing: Carnegie-Tsinghua Center for Global Policy. Available at http://carnegietsinghua.org/2017/05/10/how-china-is-using-its-economic-goals-to-assert-its-global-influence-pub-69921. Accessed 20 August 2017.

Ikenberry, G. John. 2011. *Liberal Leviathan: The Origins, Crisis, and Transformation of the American World Order.* Princeton, NJ: Princeton University Press.

Kingsley, Edney. 2014. *The Globalization of Chinese Propaganda. International Power and Domestic Political Cohesion.* Basingstoke: Palgrave Macmillan.

Ministry of Foreign Affairs, Federal Democratic Republic of Ethiopia. 2014. "Ethiopia–China Relations: An Excellent Model for South-South Cooperation." http://213.55.98.12/web/guest/articles/-/asset_publisher/TiDZpSUe5oS6/content/ethiopia-china-relations-an-excellent-model-for-south-south-cooperation? Accessed 21 September 2017.

Ministry of Foreign Affairs of the People's Republic of China. 2015. "Toward a New Type of International Relations of Win-Win Cooperation." http://www.fmprc.gov.cn/mfa_eng/wjb_663304/wjbz_663308/2461_663310/t1248487.shtml.

Radelet, Steven, and Jeffrey D. Sachs. 1998. *The East Asian Financial Crisis: Diagnosis, Remedies, Prospects.* Washington, DC: Brookings Papers on Economic Activities.

US Department of State. 2016, September 28. *Secretary John Kerry Remarks on the Trans-Pacific Partnership.* Washington, DC: Wilson Center.

Xi, Jinping. 2014, May 21. "New Asian Security Concept for New Progress in Security Cooperation." Fourth Summit of the Conference on Interaction and Confidence Building Measures in Asia Shanghai. Available at http://www.fmprc.gov.cn/mfa_eng/zxxx_662805/t1159951.shtml. Accessed 23 September 2017.

Yan, Xuetong. 2014. "From Keeping a Low Profile to Striving for Achievement." *Chinese Journal of International Politics* 72 (2): 153–184.

Index

A

Agreement, 95–98, 101–108, 110–113, 125, 129
ASEAN, 8, 11, 13, 14, 16, 38, 50, 81, 95, 96, 98, 102–108, 121
ASEAN+1, 96, 106, 107
ASEAN+3, 8, 14, 96, 123
ASEAN+6, 95, 96, 102, 122
Asia, 1, 2, 4, 11, 12–17, 19, 28, 30, 35, 39, 41, 52–54, 57–59, 67–70, 79, 80, 82, 84–87, 95–98, 100–103, 105, 109, 112, 119–127, 130, 131
Asia Infrastructure Investment Bank (AIIB), 2, 9, 17, 20, 27, 38, 39, 41, 43, 47–64, 79, 80, 96, 98, 112, 119, 121, 122, 124, 126–130
Asia Pacific, 15, 17, 35, 101

B

Banking, 20, 72, 76, 77
Belt and Road Initiative (BRI), 2, 9, 17, 20, 27, 38, 41, 43, 57, 58, 61, 64, 67–71, 74–89, 96, 112, 119, 121, 122, 124–127, 130
Boundaries, 6, 9, 10, 13–15, 86, 87, 102, 123, 124
Bretton Woods system, 48

C

China, 1–4, 6–21, 25–43, 47–58, 61–64, 68–71, 73–89, 95–98, 100–105, 107, 108, 110–113, 119–131
China Dream, 27, 33–35, 42, 43, 47, 49, 50, 127
Chinese leadership, 12, 14, 19, 21, 26, 31, 33, 43, 67, 73, 80, 96, 99, 113, 120, 124, 127
Communist Party of China, 20, 32
Connectivity, 57, 58, 70, 71, 75, 78, 80, 82, 86, 88, 100, 112, 124
Constructivism, 3, 4, 7, 16, 31, 33, 35, 72, 98, 128
Contestation, 3, 4, 8, 9, 11–13, 61, 71, 86, 88, 102, 108, 120, 121, 123, 126

https://doi.org/10.1007/978-3-319-75505-2

D
Deng Xiaoping, 1, 2, 27, 34, 52
Developing countries, 28, 29, 36, 39, 41, 42, 54, 57, 64, 69, 71, 99, 103, 107, 124, 127–131
Development, 2, 3, 6, 8, 9, 12, 17–20, 30, 32, 34, 37–39, 41, 43, 48, 49, 52–55, 59–62, 64, 69–71, 78, 84, 87–89, 99–103, 106, 108, 110, 111, 113, 124, 125, 129–131
Dispute settlement mechanism, 106, 107

E
East Asia, 2, 11–17, 29, 30, 57, 96, 98, 103, 124
East-West co-governance, 54
English School, 2–7, 9, 10, 13, 15, 16, 18, 26, 39, 42, 52, 120, 125
European Union, 8, 69, 81

F
Five Principles of Peaceful Co-existence, 16, 28, 84, 99, 124
Foreign direct investments (FDI), 73, 108, 109
Foreign policy, 6, 16, 20, 26–28, 30, 33–38, 41–43, 50, 52, 57, 68, 69, 79, 84–87, 103, 120, 125, 127–130
Free trade agreement (FTAs), 43, 95, 96, 104, 106, 107, 111, 125

G
Geography, 13, 121
Global governance, 6, 8, 10, 26, 28–30, 34, 36, 38–41, 43, 48–52, 54, 55, 61, 64, 81, 98, 99, 107, 121, 127, 128, 130
Globalization, 6, 9, 19, 40, 50, 69, 77, 80, 98–101, 120, 128, 129, 131
Global order, 1, 2, 6–9, 25, 27–29, 31, 39, 42, 43, 52, 64, 70, 87, 120, 126, 130
Governance, 2, 8, 10, 13, 14, 18–20, 37, 39–42, 48, 51–55, 62–64, 69, 77, 81, 82, 87, 97–100, 106, 113, 119, 121, 123, 125, 129–131
Great power management, 5, 10–13, 61, 89, 121, 122
Great powers, 2, 3, 5, 6, 10, 11, 14, 27, 30, 35–37, 39, 55, 57, 64, 70, 78, 87, 89, 120–123, 129

H
Harmony, 33, 39, 40, 70, 101, 108, 113, 129
Hu Jintao, 2, 121

I
India, 29, 59, 79, 82–85, 96, 105, 111, 112, 122, 125
Infrastructure, 2, 38, 47, 48, 50, 52, 53, 55, 57–59, 63, 64, 68–71, 74, 75–77, 80, 82, 86, 88, 89, 119, 125, 126
Institutions, 4, 6, 8, 11, 15, 27, 38–43, 48–57, 61, 63, 64, 69, 77, 86, 120, 121, 123, 126, 130
Intellectual property (IP), 102, 105, 106, 109, 125
International financial Institutions (IFIs), 40, 41, 43, 47–50, 53, 54, 57, 63, 64, 77, 123
International Monetary Fund, 48

International order, 3–7, 9, 10, 16, 18, 19, 21, 26, 30, 38, 39, 42, 43, 50–52, 56, 80, 82, 98, 100, 120, 124, 129
International society, 2, 4, 7, 8, 10, 13–15, 17, 18, 35
Investments, 48, 52, 55–58, 62, 71, 73–76, 78, 80–82, 84, 85, 88, 96, 99, 102, 103, 106, 107, 109, 110, 125, 126
Investment Settlement Dispute Mechanism (ISDM), 110

J
Japan, 11, 12, 14, 15, 18, 37, 49, 79, 83, 84, 95–96, 104, 105, 112, 122, 124
Jiang Zemin, 2, 14

L
Leaders, 2, 9, 11, 12, 14, 26–28, 31–34, 36, 38–40, 42, 43, 49, 51, 52, 56, 68, 69, 71, 75, 81, 98, 100, 102, 113, 120, 124, 127–129
Liberalism, 2, 3, 18–20, 35, 39, 51, 53, 58, 73, 80–82, 96, 99, 104, 105, 112, 120, 131

M
Market, 5, 6, 10, 17–20, 40–42, 58, 61, 62, 71–74, 76, 77, 79, 88, 101, 103, 105, 108–110, 121–123, 125–127
Marxism, 32–34, 36, 42
Myanmar, 60, 79, 85, 86, 95, 108

N
Narrative, 2, 7, 21, 26–35, 37, 38, 41, 42, 49–54, 56, 57, 62–64, 67–71, 81, 87, 98, 100, 101, 108, 113, 121, 124, 127–130
Nationalism, 5, 15, 21, 27–30, 34, 50, 69, 98, 128
Neo-Confucianism, 15, 21, 27, 41, 49, 50, 69, 98
New type of great powers relations, 36
A new type of international institutions, 27, 39, 42
Non interference, 5, 8, 15, 17, 30, 48, 52, 54, 70, 80, 82, 84, 85, 87, 107, 124, 125, 128, 130
Non tariff barriers, 19, 20, 96, 97, 125

O
Obama, Barack, 15, 37, 79, 96, 102, 110, 122, 127
Outbound direct investments (ODI), 73, 107, 109, 126
Over production, 76

P
Pakistan, 60, 62, 63, 79, 83, 85, 125
Pluralist/Pluralism, 5, 6, 8–10, 10, 16, 17, 19, 20, 26, 42, 52, 53, 61, 77, 78, 80–82, 87–89, 97, 104, 107, 110, 123, 124, 126, 130
Post-colonial, 8, 15, 16, 21, 27–29, 33, 34, 42, 49, 50, 53, 57, 63, 64, 69, 70, 87, 98, 100, 113, 127, 128
Power transition, 2, 29, 51
Primary institutions, 1, 4, 5, 7, 8, 10, 11, 13–15, 17, 18, 61, 71, 86, 88, 89, 108, 120, 124, 126

R
Realism, 36, 37
Region, 3, 8–15, 17, 29, 30, 38, 39, 48, 50, 52–55, 57, 58, 63, 64, 70, 76, 78–81, 84–89, 97, 101, 102, 122–125
Regional Comprehensive Economic Partnership (RCEP), 2, 9, 17, 20, 27, 39, 41, 43, 61, 79, 80, 95–98, 101–113, 119, 121–127, 129, 130
Regional Investment Bank, 53
Regionalism, 16, 52, 86, 96, 123, 127
Regional order, 2–4, 7–15, 17, 20, 21, 48, 50, 70, 71, 77, 79, 80, 86, 88, 97, 107, 108, 121–126
Responsibility to Protect, 6
Rules of origin (ROOs), 96, 103–105
Russia, 28, 29, 37, 38, 80, 82, 83, 125

S
Solidarism, 9, 97, 106, 108
South Korea, 12, 18, 48, 83, 84, 96, 105, 124
Sovereign state, 17, 19, 58
Sovereignty, 5, 6, 8, 10, 14–17, 19, 20, 26, 28–30, 39, 42, 48, 52, 54, 58, 61, 62, 80, 82–85, 87, 88, 97, 99, 104, 106, 107, 110, 111, 113, 121, 123–125, 128, 130
State Asset Supervision and Administration Commission (SASAC), 72, 74, 75, 109
State capitalism, 17, 19, 61–63, 70, 71, 76, 77, 82, 88, 89, 109, 110, 123, 126
State owned enterprises (SOEs), 58, 62, 63, 71–77, 85, 88, 97, 108–111, 113, 125–127

T
Thucydides's trap, 29, 49
Trade, 3, 6, 10, 19, 29, 40, 70, 76, 77, 79, 83, 87, 96–100, 102–113, 120, 125, 129
Trans Pacific Partnership (TPP), 15, 19, 96–98, 101–104, 106, 108–113, 123, 125–127
Trump, Donald, 49, 80, 84, 98, 100, 111, 122, 123, 131

U
United States (US), 2, 3, 9, 11–15, 17, 25, 31, 32, 35–38, 42, 48–52, 55, 59, 60, 73, 76, 77, 79, 80, 84, 87, 96–101, 106, 109, 110, 112, 113, 120, 122–124, 126, 127, 130, 131

W
World Economic Forum, 40, 99

X
Xi Jinping, 1, 2, 10, 14, 26, 27, 31–38, 41, 42, 50, 52, 56–58, 62, 64, 68, 69, 99, 119, 120, 127, 128

Z
Zhu Rongji, 71, 75

The manufacturer's authorised representative in the EU is Springer Nature Customer Service Centre GmbH, Europaplatz 3, 69115 Heidelberg, Germany. If you have any concerns regarding our products, please contact ProductSafety@springernature.com

Printed and bound by CPI Group (UK) Ltd, Croydon, CR0 4YY
05/10/2026
02228161-0001